Endocellular Selection

Evolution without Darwin

John A. Rush

Published by Amazon

ISBN: 979-8486707162

Table of Contents

Preface

Darwinian evolution contains two concepts, both of which have been overstated in their importance for the origin of species. The first is that new species come about through random, without purpose alterations in genetic coding, in slow, incremental steps, over long periods of time. The second is the idea of natural selection, a numbers game, where those that produce the greatest numbers of offspring and pass on their genes are the most "fit." One mechanism offered for natural selection is sexual selection, behind which is a conscious actor (a bug, cat, or human) thus nullifying the concept as random, at least for sexual selection. Out of these numbers, Nature, in short, culls the "unfit" leaving the fit survivors to carry on the next generation. So, the survival of the fittest are the ones that survive. There is really nothing to see here as we are dealing with a circular argument – those that survive are the most fit, and the most fit are the ones that survive. It's like saying "God created everything, everything was created by God." This really tells us nothing; there is no proof to be found in a circular argument. In science, circular arguments don't hold much weight, with one exception, the Darwinian formula.

In the pages to follow I show, with a brief look at research over many decades, that random mutations and natural selection, if important at all, have only a minor part to play in the stages of life. Scientists have been aware of the limitations of the Darwinian model for over 150 years, yet the model persists, and those not "buying in," have been treated very badly; shame on the academic community. What has been left out of the equation is the cell's will to survive and to do that the cell needs to take an active part in its evolution, or what I call *endocellular selection*. To suggest that random mutations are the only method of altering coding sequences limits our thinking and the consideration of other possibilities. Environmental stressors represent *information only* to which the cell responds and then alters coding sequences directly; this is not random but occurs with thinking and decision making at the cellular and quantum levels.

Moreover, it appears that cells think ahead and plan for the future. Because the future can't be known cells make mistakes; certain situations can't be anticipated, like catastrophic events, or as in the Dutch Hunger study, a lack of nutrients was interpreted by the cells as low caloric availability after parturition. This led to overindulgence and obesity in the next generation. As another example, millions of years ago we turned off the enzyme uricase, necessary for removing uric acid from the blood (we now remove it through our kidneys). Uric acid circulating in the blood apparently allowed our ancestors to store fat (converted from fructose) which could be used as an energy source when the seasons changed and fruit (fructose) was not available (the human animal is the only primate with a layer of fat under the skin). In today's world, with ample food available in industrialized nations, this has led to high incidences of type-2 diabetes. Your cells could not have anticipated this. One has to wonder, with this ability to alter coding sequences, what are our cells preparing us for in the future?

In the pages to follow I repeat basic ideas in each chapter as part of a review and to make sure the reader understands what I am conveying and to make different points. Repetition is one part of presenting and anchoring in ideas, as is the case with Darwinism, a story told over and over again as truth but without scientific validation. I also consider the part myth and our small group nature play in perpetuating a storyline as scientific when clearly it is not. Before beginning let me offer a story, the significance of which will become apparent to the reader as the chapters unfold.

The Story of the Easter Ham

Once there was a family, who lived in a small village in Ireland, the land of legends and lore. This particular family observed all the important holidays, certainly St. Patrick's Day, the monthly Bank Holidays, St. Stephen's Day, and so on. Ritual observance was very,

very important. But their most favorite holidays were Christmas and Easter. Christmas was always a joy, with the kids making cookies, talking with Grandma and Grandpa, telling stories, and enjoying good food. The other important day was Easter for this was Grandma's day, a ritual tradition for her, where she cooked the Easter ham. The ham, about 12 pounds, was neatly prepared by first cutting off the ends of the ham, special herbs were applied, and it was placed in its special pan, the one her grandma used, those many years ago. This was a long tradition going back many generations.

This year Grandma was being helped by her granddaughter, Ciara, who was aged four years. She didn't have much experience in cooking but was fascinated with Grandma's skill in preparing the ham. Grandpa often helped place the ham in the oven for it was heavy and would take several hours to cook. All the while Ciara asked question; she was the inquisitive one.

Ciara: "Grandma, why did you sprinkle that stuff on the ham?"

Grandma: "To give it more flavor, my dear."

Ciara: "Why are there strings around the ham? Is this so it can't get away?"

Grandma: "No, my dear," she said with a smile. "It's to keep the flavors in."

Ciara: "Why did you cut the ends of the ham? Will you cook these differently?"

Grandma: "I cut the ends off, just like my mother did, and her mother before her, and her mother before her, so as to keep the meat moist and sweet."

With that Grandpa began to snicker which rolled into a good belly laugh.

Grandma looked at Grandpa and asked, "What in the *world* are you laughing at?"

Grandpa: "Well, I knew your Grandmother, as you well know, although I was young, and I asked her the same question."

Grandma: "Well, what did she tell you?"

Grandpa: "She cut the ends of the ham because your grandfather, God rest his soul, was too cheap to buy a larger pan for the large hams he brought home!"

With this, Grandpa left the room, still laughing under his breath.

I want to thank Nick Caya, Mary, and associates at Word-2-Kindle for cover art, final formatting, and editing.

John A. Rush

Fall 2021

CHAPTER 1

Introduction

IF there is one thing that undermines Darwinian evolution, that is, the insistence that random mutations and natural selection are the singular keys to the origins of life and species, it would be the cell's ability to "think," make decisions, and alter its DNA accordingly. This idea is implied in the works of Jean-Baptiste Lamarck (1809) and it resurfaced as "directed mutation" by Cairns et al. (1988). The cell's active participation (instead of a passive recipient) in its evolution-ary direction is unthinkable for many researchers mainly because it undermines randomness and natural selection and extends change potential to the cell itself. How much of biological evolution is ran-dom and how much is directed or purposefully initiated by the cell? How does this relate to consciousness and the cell's ability to "think," make decisions, and alter its DNA? These are large issues.

Information theory demands a sender and receiver. In this case, the environment represents information that is received by organic life and then acted upon by those lifeforms. Some information is injurious to lifeforms, for example, UV radiation, and toxins from plants and industry that can alter coding sequences. Much of the information we sense, however, is interpreted as stressful to one degree or another, as examples, cold stress, the neighbor's dog, or driving a car. It is these stressors that are detected and responded to by the cell.

External events (the environment) do not pick and choose genes or fine-tune anything; the environment (herein called

Nature), in most cases, is *information only*; the cell has to decide what to do with this information which, in a large sense, again, equals *stress* (nutritional, toxin, temperature, etc.). When I read a book, the book doesn't do anything to me, although I may alter my thought patterns and behavior – I decide to do this, the book is information only and decides nothing. Even the admission of cells controlling DNA, as in epigenetics, has to be avoided least someone ask, "Well, how much is random and how much is decided by the cell?

Nature, in this metaphor, represents death (entropy) to which the cell has to react or die, and if life were merely at the mercy of Nature's whims, without any say in the matter, there would be no life. Life, in all probability, can only alter or extinguish itself sometimes by making bad decisions.

Clarification

I'm starting off with a number of definitions. These definitions have been bent and stretched in many directions over the years, so, for clarity:

Evolution – This is the alteration of coding sequences (genotype) leading to both phenotypic or expressed differences between species as well as the development of new genus and species. Before you can have biological evolution, you need lifeforms. The origin of life at this point in our science is a mystery and cannot be accounted for by random chance or natural selection. Just saying it is so, over and over again, without scientific proof, does not make it true.

Gene – A gene usually incorporates a number of different coding sequences at diverse points on the DNA code. I use the term *coding sequences* to include all sequences necessary for gene expression.

Functioning Protein – A functioning protein is one that will fold properly (amino acids all have to be L- or left handed), and then used, in some manner *in conjunction with other functional proteins*, in lifeforms on this planet. Considering all the possibilities, lifeforms on planet Earth use very few functional proteins.

Epigenetics – This is the addition or subtraction of chemical elements from DNA and histones and has the effect of decreasing or increasing the expression of a gene (much more detail is offered in Chapter 3). Epigenetics, or cell generated alterations in genetic coding sequences, is a scientifically verifiable process that could lead, over time, in the same manner as Darwin's slow incremental changes, to the origin of new species. The Darwinian model of chance happenings is of minor importance. Chance does play a part, but life, or the *continuation* of life, leaves little to chance; life always finds a way and to slow down entropy, life has to stay ahead of death – chance happenings can lead to death.

Symbiosis – Life has an affinity for life and one quasi-life form, the virus, has been on our planet from the beginning and has greatly influenced the origin of new, very different species. Human DNA contains approximately 100,000 pieces of viral DNA, making up about *eight to ten percent* of the human genome, and this is a great deal of information. The addition of new information is a key to the origin of species and this can happen rapidly. The Darwinians emphatically state that developing new species is a gradual, incremental affair, and, considering epigenetics and endocellular selection, this is true for the most part. A good example of rapid change is the viral influence on the development of the placenta which occurred between 80 and 120 million years ago. We go from being Theria (marsupials) to Eutheria (modern mammals), one genus and species to another, with the help of a virus in a very short time, perhaps one generation. This is called symbiosis, where a totally different lifeform contributes new DNA to another lifeform.

Simply put, symbiosis is the combining of life forms. As mentioned above, the placenta of Eutheria mammals is the product of a virus seeking immortality through incorporating itself into tissue that would secure its passage into the next generation. The mitochondria in eukaryotes (multi-celled lifeforms) appears to be from bacteria (archaea) that invaded other bacteria adding its genetic material securing its place in the future.

Viruses have likely been invading bacteria since lifeforms emerged in this universe. Bacteria and viruses have coexisted on this planet for billions of years. Bacteria can replicate themselves; viruses (as far as I know) need a self-replicating lifeform in order to duplicate themselves. And, initially, that would be bacteria. Over long periods of time the bacteria learned to defend themselves against viral attack; we have inherited many of these immune factors, but there is always a new virus on the block. Viruses may not be able to duplicate themselves, *but they can change their characteristics* (alter their coding sequences) when confronted by, for example, immune factors. We are seeing this with COVID-19 and the new strain from India (strain D, and there are other strains to come – this is not the work of randomness; the virus wants immortality and that is unlikely to happen randomly). This type of thinking, that is, alterations to coding sequences are random, has likely held up our ability to protect ourselves form bacteria and viruses; dealing with an adversary that thinks is much different than dealing with one that doesn't. Dealing with a rock is one thing; dealing with the rattlesnake under the rock is another. So, bacteria serve to continue "life" *for* the virus, and the bacteria get new information *from* viruses; this is a give and take.

Hybridization – Animals of the same species, having been separated for long periods of time, can mate and produce, if not new species, diversity in coding sequences. Neanderthals, according to the genomic studies, do not have the diversity as found in modern humans. Our diversity is attributed to hybridization, especially with modern humans coming back into Africa around 300 KYA and hybridizing with the different Homo groups existing throughout the continent. This hybridization and collecting diversity may be one of the reasons we are still around and Neanderthals, Denisovans, and other ancient ancestors went extinct. Is hybridization random? No, not when you have lifeforms – lifeforms aren't rocks, they making decisions. And the fact that bobcats search for other bobcats with whom to mate, and not the farmer's dog – I think you get the point.

Endocellular Selection – Thinking and decision making occur at the cellular level including alterations to coding sequences; it is cellular communication and decision making that prompts epigenetic alteration of the DNA code, as well as other types of alterations (see mutations below), and these can be passed on to the next generation especially when enacted in utero. This is contrary to natural selection but a major mechanism, in my opinion, connected to Lamarck's acquired inherited characteristics. Cairns, et all. (1988) call this "directed mutation," which caused a great deal of controversy. (See, for example, Anderson et al. 2011 for critique, and there are others online.) The issue for Cairns was *Escherichia coli* finding itself in a lactose environment, not able to digest that type of sugar. After a short while a phase shift occurred (lac operon – this may be related to quantum tunneling) and genes are altered allowing it to digest lactose rather than glucose. The scientists critiquing the research by Cairn, et al. suggest, instead, that the ability was already available (a preadaptation) in a small portion of the *E. coli* sample, indicating, of course, that *only* random mutations and natural selection were in play and not the intent of the bacteria. *Perhaps the "preadaptation" was directed by the cell in its need to anticipate the future and stay ahead of Nature* – more on this in Chapter 2.

Cairns's result contradicted the well-established principle that mutations occurred randomly; his experiments appeared to demonstrate that mutations tended to occur *when they were advantageous.* The findings appeared to support the discredited Lamarckian theory of evolution – the starved bacteria weren't growing long necks but, just like Lamarck's imaginary antelope, they appeared to be responding to an environmental challenge by generating heritable modifications: mutations.

Cairns's experimental finding were soon confirmed by several other scientists. Yet the phenomenon had no explanation within contemporary genetics and molecular biology. There was simply no known mechanism that would allow a bacterium, or indeed any creature, to choose which genes to mutate and when. The finding also appeared to contradict what someone called the central dogma of molecular biology: the principle that information flows only one way during transcription, from DNA out to the proteins to the environment of a cell or organism. If Cairns's results were right, then cells must be also capable of reversing the flow of genetic information, allowing the environment [cell] to influence what is written in the DNA (McFadden and Al-Khalili 2014: 221-222). (emphasis mine)

Another problem I see with those who contend that natural selection is in play is the definition of "fitness." Unless we have a clear, specific definition we can't be sure what the researchers are measuring as the survivors may not be "fit" in terms of survival into the next generation.

Epigenetics would also appear to negate the critics in the sense that the cell is making the changes to its DNA and histones – this is an example of *specificity* and not part of the random mutation mantra. One of the basic issues, again, is defining "fitness" (see below).

Natural Selection – This refers to reproductive success. This is also where Nature culls out the unfit and fine-tunes biological systems with organisms being passive recipients of what Nature throws at it. In other words, and according to the Darwinians, the environment is in charge of evolution and the cell has little or no say. The external world, however, can only offer information; natural selection does not create or alter coding sequences. Darwin (2019: 197) makes a comparison between the human breeding practices of game-cocks with Nature performing in a similar manner. He writes (2019: 197):

> Just as man can improve the breeds of his game-cocks by the selection of those birds which are victorious in the cockpit, so it appears that the strongest and most vigorous males, or those provided with the best weapons, have prevailed under nature, and have led to the improvement of the natural breed or species.

The problem here is that improving breeds by *human* design is not arbitrary but specific. Natural selection, on the other hand, is haphazard and by chance. Mother Nature is blind. Moreover, stating that natural selection promotes fitness is the same as saying those that survive are the most fit. This is a circular argument. This is not allowed in science. Darwin offers no clear definition of "fit" or "fitness" other than those that survive are most fit. This is so general as to be meaningless.

Natural selection has nothing to do with specificity, of picking and choosing particular coding sequences. But, if natural selection acts the way the Darwinians believe, that is, the actions of natural selection are specific in the sense of choosing or fine-tuning a trait leading to "fitness," then an energy, an intelligence has to be involved directing the selection.

Sexual Selection, according to Darwin, is a particular type of selection specifically designed to enhance probability of producing offspring. Here Darwin is suggesting that the environment purposely targets specific characteristics when in fact Nature targets by chance, not choice. Sexual selection is selection by a *conscious entity* which is quite unlike indifferent Nature. For Darwin, sexual selection is how natural selection works. With cells thinking and deciding one has to ponder, which is more likely to lead to survival in the future, natural selection or the cell thinking ahead? This brings us to "consciousness" which I will discuss in Chapter 4.

Random Mutation – This is the Darwinian belief that alterations in the genetic code happen arbitrarily and without purpose, and, through slow, incremental changes, new species emerge. How random mutations can create codes has never been scientifically demonstrated.

In, *What Darwin and Dawkins Didn't Know* (2020: 39), I noted statistics that indicate the probability of random mutations creating a single, small functioning protein, *let alone a functioning cell*, during the whole age of the universe (13.8 billion years) is so incredibly low as to be impossible. This research is ignored by dedicated Darwinians.

Moreover, a functioning protein is useless without RNA, and other enzymes and coding sequences to perform some task, so we end up with a chicken and egg issue where all, out of necessity, have to show up at the same time. The probability of that happening randomly is way beyond impossible.

Mutation Types (all thought to be random; this is now questionable):

Genetic Drift – This occurs with small spelling mistakes in the coding sequences over time that then lead to phenotypic changes and new species through isolation and time. The effects are most noticeable in small populations. Is genetic drift truly random or is this the cell altering its coding sequences over time? Spelling mistakes do occur but *most* are corrected, and those that aren't could well be directed by the cell itself. This is often compared to linguistic drift, with phonemes (sound units) altered over time leading to a new language. Alterations in phonemes don't lead to the "death" or "illness" of a language; whether or not they can alter the "fitness" of the language, you would have to ask a linguist, as I'm not sure what a "fit" language would be.

Genetic drift might, in fact, be directed by the cell and not simply accidental as with linguistic drift. Somehow certain animals have the ability to "predict" the future, at least within a season or two. Squirrels, for example, will often "stock up" for an anticipated poor season. Currently in Northern California we are into our drought cycle and the squirrels that live in a tree on the property are stocking up. How do they know? This ability to predict would have high survival value for the cell/organism.

Small, incremental alterations in behavior, due to environmental changes, are transmitted to the cell and decisions have to be made to adjust to these changes in the external world *al la* Lamarck. This is not an all or nothing issue. Yes, a random alteration in a coding sequence, brought on by, for example, UV radiation, could possibly lead to alteration in phenotypes, but most point mutations don't build new proteins and are often of little significance. An example of a point mutation would be the difference between attached and unattached ear lobes. I'm not sure what the survival value of specific types of ear lobes would be. Perhaps attached ear lobes are more aesthetic and "fit;" unattached ear lobes, however, will hold more jewelry – you can take your choice here.

Transposition, or transposable element or transposon, also called jumping genes, can alter their position within a genome. By doing so they can reverse mutations and alter gene expression. They make up a great deal of the genome, and are important in the origin of species. These alterations are unlikely to be random. Cancer cells, through their complex communication patterns, can certainly do this which informs that healthy cells can manage this as well. Moreover, viruses may play an important part, especially as retrotransposons.

> . . . [S]cientists have known for some time that symbiosis occurred between bacteria and archaea, evidenced by the mitochondria in eukaryotes. Viruses have also combined with plants and animals (in humans, becoming endogenous or HERVs —human-endogenous-retro-transposons, or retrotransposons), which can lead to rapid speciation by entering new information into prokaryote or eukaryote cells (Rush 2020: 105).

Most, if not all these transpositions are carried out by enzymes *directed by the cell*. More on this later.

Missense Mutation – This is a change in one DNA base pair resulting in the substitution of one amino acid for another in the protein made by a gene. Sometimes such a substitution codes for the same protein and occurred so the protein could fold properly. This is why there is a redundancy in protein coding (see Rush 2020: 16, 34-35) and this is highly unlikely to be random.

Nonsense Mutation – This involves a change in one DNA base pair. By substituting one amino acid for another the altered DNA sequence prematurely signals the cell to stop building a protein.

This type of mutation results in a shortened protein that may function improperly or not at all. Again, random mutations can cause such alterations, but so can healthy and cancerous cells.

Insertion – Insertions change the number of DNA bases in a gene by adding a piece of DNA. As a result, the protein made by the gene may not function properly. Not all insertions, however, are deleterious. A problem lies with knowing which are random and which are cell directed.

Deletion – Deletions change the number of DNA bases by removing a piece of DNA. Small deletions may remove one or a few base pairs within a gene; larger deletions can remove an entire gene or several neighboring genes. The deleted DNA may alter the function of the resulting protein(s) and this doesn't always appear to lead to disease states. Again, random mutations from toxic chemicals, etc. can cause such alterations, but so can healthy and cancerous cells.

Duplication – Duplication consists of a piece of DNA that is copied (this may be purposeful and not abnormal) one or more times. This type of alteration can modify the function of the resulting protein. A sequence connected to cortical brain parts in genome of humans is duplicated *212 times* as compared to 37 times in chimps. What are the chances of a random, indiscriminate, unintentional, accidental mutation occurring with respect to the same coding sequence 212 times? The chances are as close to impossible as you can get. The fact that there is a difference between chimps and humans suggests the cells in the human animal are more actively selecting for intelligence at least since the Miocene (23-6 MYA), so this wasn't simply a one-time mutation/alteration in the coding sequences.

Frameshift Mutation – Mutations occur when the addition or loss of DNA bases changes a gene's reading frame. A reading frame consists of groups of 3 bases that each code for one amino acid. A frameshift mutation shifts the grouping of these bases and changes the code for amino acids. The resulting protein is sometimes nonfunctional. However, as mentioned earlier, *E. coli* can "flip" a switch and go from consuming glucose to digesting lactose (lac operon). In the case of yeast, they can flip a switch and go from utilizing glucose as an energy source, to utilizing ethanol. Bacteria and yeast can think and decide; they have to stay ahead of Nature and natural selection through their own internal modifications. Some modifications lead to the demise of the genes for sure, but doing *something* might be better than doing nothing at all. Quantum tunneling may be connected to this process.

Repeat Expansion – Nucleotide repeats are short DNA sequences that are repeated a number of times in a row. For example, a trinucleotide repeat is made up of 3-base-pair sequences, and a tetranucleotide repeat is made up of 4-base-pair sequences. A repeat expansion is an alteration that increases the number of times that the short DNA sequence is repeated. This type of alteration can sometimes cause the resulting protein to function improperly, but appears too specific to be random, and might be responsible for the 3rd opsin allowing us to see the world in color. In each case, how can one determine the change factor involved a random alteration or is it, instead, endocellular selection?

Staying with mutations for the moment, the current problem is determining when these types of alterations (and others) happen randomly and when the *cell* is prompting the changes. One way to go about this is to determine if the alteration leads to disease. Because most spelling mistakes are corrected, don't disrupt cellular functioning, and are recessive, in my opinion, those alterations that lead to disease are random mutations mainly caused by exposure to toxins (industrial byproducts, toxins in foods, tobacco use, constipation, UV radiation, gamma rays, solar flares, etc.). Because some of these alterations occur so frequently – especially transposition, these seem to be choices and not chance.

Cells can make bad decisions, particularly under stress, that can likewise lead to disease, particularly in the next generation.

The Generic – As I have suggested elsewhere (Rush 2020: 113, 184), life would appear to have a default system, or life forms that live through and continue to exist after catastrophic events. The three major life forms that fit this description are bacteria (aerobic and anaerobic), archaea (a type of bacteria that produces methane), and viruses. But the generic extends way past this. The generic is a irreducibly complex base platform that, once constructed, can be added onto or epigenetically modified to fit prevailing environmental conditions. For example, once you have a functioning tooth this can be modified epigenetically in many ways to fit the needs of the cell or organism in its food quest.

Chemical Evolution – Before you can have anything like natural selection, there has to be a life form(s) to select. The original life forms on planet Earth, and how they came about, has been attributed to chemistry, i.e. the attraction of inorganic and organic chemicals hypothesized to be present in the oceans of early Earth. There are numerous models and experiments in the literature carried out since the early 1950s. None of the experiments (see Thaxton et al. 1986 and 2020) have given rise to anything resembling self-replicating life forms, and those that show promise are due to *experimenter interference*, not natural, random processes. As an example, laboratory experiments reveal it is easy to create amino acids. However, they always form as both right handed and left handed (racemic), never exclusively R- or L-. The amino acids that service life on planet Earth are L- or left handed, and I have not encountered anything in the literature that proves the spontaneous production of only L- amino acids in laboratory experiments outside of experimenter interference. Saying it *could* have happened is okay as an hypothesis but not as a fact. As mentioned, only L-handed amino acids service life on planet Earth because, if there is a mixture of R- and L-, the probability of the protein folding properly is next to zero, and if it doesn't fold up properly it is nonfunctional.

Metaphysics – This refers to discussions of cause and effect that go way beyond classical physics. The multi-verse, the self-assembly of life, string theory, parts of quantum mechanics, and so on, are allowed, of course; we need ideas to test. The problem lies in selling these ideas to students and the public at large as *truth*. Darwinian evolution, in this sense, is metaphysical, as the ability for new species to form through random mutations of the DNA code and natural selection are suppositions, opinions, or metaphysics verging on the magical but have been marketed and sold as truth; questioning this "truth" is not allowed. The lack of critical thinking in the arena of evolution is troublesome. Science should be "open," not closed; dogma and science are polar opposites.

Space Aliens, Panspermia, and Intelligent Design – The storyline of aliens from other worlds coming to planet Earth and manipulating genes doesn't help us much either. Sitchin (1995), one of the originators of this storyline, uses ancient Sumerian myths, and so on, to weave a story of aliens who come to Earth and genetically altered one of our close ancestors, perhaps Neanderthals, producing us. We are then used as slaves mining gold, etc. This may or may not be true but it doesn't provide information on the original development of life forms.

Panspermia centers on the idea that life did not start on planet Earth but somewhere else in the early universe, on another planet perhaps, which was destroyed sending material, including bacteria, etc., to distant areas of the universe. Some scientists (see Thaxton et al. 2020: 386) believe this an unlikely scenario because even spore forming bacteria would be destroyed by UV radiation. However, Aron and Grossman (2013) report that one of the best shields against radiation is water – thus the use of human excrement in the shielding of space craft.

Bacteria (or other dormant life forms) in comets, space objects made up of ice and dirt, however, would be protected for long periods in space. So, this is a possibility. But, this does not inform as to how these life forms emerged in the first place.

Because of the complexity of life forms, and the inability to duplicate life under laboratory conditions, this has led some researchers to suspect there is an intelligence behind the origins of life on this planet and perhaps the universe. In other words, there "seems" to be an intelligence at work, *not that there is*. The Darwinians dogmatically contend life and new species only occur randomly and are overseen by natural selection, period. Any doubters are obviously religious freaks. Intelligent Design has nothing to do with religion, for religion involves worship enacted by ritual, which is not part of Intelligent Design. There is no Church of Intelligent Design, no non-profit status, and no personalized god suggested or implied. Moreover, if there is an intelligence behind the origins of life, the methods of creating life are not magical, although the complexity and super intelligence necessary to create life might appear that way. This, however, is simply a product of our ignorance. Because Intelligent Design has been labeled "religion" by the Darwinians I use the terms *congruent construction* (Rush 2020: 5, 85) to avoid any connection to religion or religious practices. To me the origin and complexity of the perceived universe is an enigma and that is as far as I'm willing to go.

CHAPTER 2

The Problem

WITH the origins of life being the first problem, the second problem involves the processes or the manner in which biological evolution occurs. We can see in the paleontological record, after each catastrophic event in prehistory, new animals and plants emerge. Without such evidence from the past we could assume that plants and animals existing today have never changed and have been in place since the beginning. The Greeks were one of the first to suggest that in the past animals were bigger and stronger. This was the golden age epitomized by the Titans. Then there was the Silver Age, the Bronze Age, and so on where we go from being giants to what we see today. Ovid (43 BCE – 17/18 CE), a Roman poet, saw this in a social, technological sense as well as offering a moral statement with the Golden Age being one of peace and justice, to the Iron Age where greed and warfare are paramount and morality almost non-existent. My guess is that Ovid, alive today, would say we are still in the Iron Age, or perhaps the "Rust" Age.

The Bible brings us a more modern concept of evolution in that there was a beginning (the "Big Bang" – recent cosmological studies indicate there was a beginning and the universe we experience has a starting point – see Meyer 2021) and the content of the universe was put in place, not all at once, but over a specific time span, that is six days (remember, the seventh day the deity rested). And if you read the *first* creation story in Genesis 1:1-31 (the second creation story is about politics and putting women on the bottom), you will recognize a sequence very much like modern science. When it comes to plants and animals, however, they are created all at once in the forms we see today. Humans are created last, man and woman, in the image of the deity, in their present form. Although still adhered to today in certain religions traditions, by the eighteenth-century literal translation of the Bible was giving way to questions from at least two camps. First, there were the paleontologists and geologists who began finding bones of huge beasts and other unrecognizable animals in different stratigraphic levels. The second came from anatomy and classification especially that of Carl Linnaeus' binomial system, and the similarities and dissimilarities between animals, past and present. This created a problem, a heretical questioning of creation as projected in Christian dogma. One of the key proponents of evolutionary thinking was Dr. Erasmus Darwin (1731-1802), an elite, Charles Darwin's grandfather.

In the Beginning . . .

I need, at this point, to again inform the reader about evolution from the Darwinian perspective and why certain beliefs are maintained in spite of massive amounts of contrary information. To begin, Charles Darwin, in 1859, published his monumental work, *The Origin of Species*. There are two basic concepts that emerge from this work. First, that species change incrementally over long periods of time into new species. These changes occur randomly and without purpose or intent.

The second concept was natural selection, or the belief that the more "fit" members of a species produce more offspring than the unfit, and those genes or traits go marching on. The "unfit" are culled by natural selection. More on this below.

Darwin's research with finches on the Galapagos Island chain convinced him that the environment, Nature, chooses characteristics best suited for the food quest (beak shape), while culling out the rest. The different finches on the various islands had different beaks for exploiting some specific niche or food source. Any "creation" involved was caused by *external Nature alone* bending and shaping the means of caloric intake. Darwin considered these different looking finches different species. We now know that the shape of the beak, and other phenotypic changes, are epigenetic in origin and, in fact, the finches are likely all one species. As Noble (2017: 123), discussing Darwin's finches, states:

> In this connection it is interesting to note that the genetic and epigenetic analysis has now been done on the Galapagos finches. The results show that at least as many epigenetic as genetic changes underlie the differences between the various species and that the number of epigenetic changes correlates rather better with evolutionary distance between the species than do the genetic changes (Skinner et al., 2014). *At the least this result puts the standard explanation for speciation in doubt in this iconic example.* From the experimental information alone, it would be impossible to say whether epigenetic changes led the speciation with subsequent assimilation into the genetic material or vice versa. Both would be possible. Even more likely, the two naturally go together. (emphasis mine)

In his last sentence I think Noble was trying to appease the Darwinians somewhat, with, "the two naturally go together," although this is unlikely to be true, unless random events can create codes. In any event, the idea of slow, incremental changes in the development of new species is a good idea. It was a breakaway from the creation dogma, of species being zapped into place by a deity of sorts, in the course of a very busy six-day period, as expressed in Genesis. But, there are many problems with Darwin's model, one of which was pointed out by Michael Behe in 1996. It is called *irreducible complexity*. In short, some systems, like a cell, blood clotting systems, the citrus acid cycle, and so on, can't function properly or function at all unless all the parts are in place – they can't be built incrementally. As Darwin (1988 [orig. 1859]: 154) stated:

> If it could be demonstrated that any complex organ existed which could not possibly have been formed by numerous,

successive, slight modifications, my theory would absolutely break down.

In 1996, Behe (2006: 39 – see Behe's latest work [2020] where he answers his critics) "broke" Darwin's process of evolution: "A single system composed of several well-matched, interacting parts that contribute to the basic function, wherein the removal of any part causes the system to effectively cease functioning . . . because any precursor to an irreducibly complex system that is missing a part is by definition nonfunctional."

In other words, irreducibly complex systems seem to just "show up" without precedents. Where do they originate? Where are the intermediate forms? According to Behe, intermediate forms can't function so they don't exist. Thus, the idea of a random, incremental development process is no longer a viable explanation for the origin of species. Keep in mind platforms (irreducibly complex systems) can be built onto, some more so than others. Teeth, for example, can exhibit great variability, but this would not be the case for a locking out knee joint. Many if not all the incremental changes we see in the paleontological record, for example, a water living amphibian spending time on land, begin with epigenetic choices, or purposeful alterations to a *generic*, functioning structure (in place since the beginning of fish, c. 400 MYA; see Shubin 2020 or his, *Your Inner Fish*, series), and not mutations in the Darwinian sense. As long as epigenetic/ phenotypic alterations do not inhibit or impair functionality there are lots of possibilities as evidenced in the paleontological record. There are many examples of irreducibly complex systems and to date no one has been able to realistically prove Behe incorrect. Yockey (2005: 181), however, surprisingly, if I read him correctly, suggests that the DNA code is *not* irreducibly complex. But, regards to specific coding sequences and the proteins involved, altering or removing bases (nucleotides) can render the sequence nonfunctional.

Again, Darwin had a good idea but his knowledge base didn't allow for irreducible complexity. Keep clearly in mind that Darwin was working with the technology of his day, so he can be excused. He didn't have access to electron microscopes, genomics, and so on, and the data accumulating over the past fifty years or so tells us a very different story. However, there is no excuse for the continued acceptance, by politicians and academics, of Darwin's opinions as fact. I have more to say about this in Chapter 6.

Natural Selection

The second hypothesis offered by Darwin, and briefly mentioned above, is "natural selection." This is a numbers game based on the idea that those with the most offspring will go marching on generation after generation. This is where Nature culls out the fit from the unfit. Even Darwin had some reservation about this. He writes (2019 [orig. 1871]):

> A most important obstacle by civilized countries to an increase in a number of men of a *superior class* has been strongly insisted upon . . . namely, the fact that the very poor and reckless, who are often degraded by vice, almost invariably marry early, whilst the careful and frugal, who are generally otherwise virtuous, marry late in life, as so they may be able to support themselves and their children in comfort. Those who marry early produce within a given period not only a greater number of generations but . . . they produce many more children. The children, moreover, that are borne by mothers during prime of life are heavier and larger, and therefore probably more vigorous, than those borne at other periods. Thus, the reckless, degraded, and often vicious members of society, tend to increase at a quicker rate than the provident and generally virtuous members. Or as Mr. Greg puts the case: *"The careless, squalid, unaspiring Irishman multiplies like rabbits: the frugal, foreseeing, self-respecting, ambitious Scot, stern in his morality, spiritual in his faith, sagacious and disciplined in his intelligence, passes his best years in struggle and in celibacy, marries late, and leaves few behind. . . . ."* (emphasis mine)

I think the reader can see where Darwin is going with this. Not only is he highly prejudiced against all outside the Anglo-Saxon "strain," with the Irish as a prime example of "reckless, degraded, and often vicious members of society," he obviously saw people fitting into different classes – he, of course, is of the "upper class." His statements echo that of Francis Galton (1822-1911) and others offering eugenics as a way to solve the problem, a way to deal with the unfit. Vlad the Impaler (c. 1428-1477), the inspiration for Dracula, had his special way of dealing with the poor, lower, degraded classes – he murdered them.

What is "Fitness?"

What does it mean to be "fit?" Strictly speaking, reproductive success. If selection means more babies then, according to his example above, the lower classes should be the most fit. Darwin and most of his colleagues knew very little about culture or cultural development, but his books most likely influenced the work of Lewis Henry Morgan. Morgan (1877) wrote a book, *Ancient Society*, wherein he outlined different stages of cultural development labeled savagery, barbarism, and civilization, emphasizing that matrilineal clans were the earliest, identifiable group organization. Many of these early ideas of social development are to be found in the works of Karl Marx and Friedrich Engels and most have been proven incorrect, insensitive, immoral, or extremely ethnocentric. However, these beliefs lit the fire for academics and those politically inspired by implying that the fit were the elite and they are the ones who should create the rules of living, least we become corrupted by the immoral and vicious lower classes (anyone not white/Anglo-Saxon, rich, politically connected, or a graduate of some prestigious institution). History shows us that the elite tend to be the *most* corrupt, immoral, and vicious.

Again, at Darwin's time in history, and even to this day, there is a belief that it is the superior, the elite, the philosophers, the scholars, those in power who are most fit, and it is this elite who should set the laws and rules because they are, for the most part, more virtuous, and so on. So, Darwin's idea of natural selection for building species turns into the Myth of the Elite, a *cultural* construction (as are all myths), of "survival of the fittest," coined by Herbert Spencer (1862).

Inherited Acquired Characteristics

Anyone with a knowledge of the history of the development of current evolutionary theory will be struck with the similarities between Darwin's thinking and that of Jean-Baptiste Lamarck (1744-1829) and his concept of inheritance of acquired characteristics. Talking about physical characteristics of sailors and others of various occupations, and the use or disuse of specific aspects of the body, he states (Darwin 2019: 34):

> Whether the several foregoing modifications would become hereditary, if the same habits of life were followed during many generations, is not known, *but it is probable*. (emphasis mine)

Darwin, however, didn't pursue this path, and on page 39 he brings up the idea of uterine development. He states, ". . . it is difficult to believe, though perhaps not impossible, that the two simple, minute, primitive tubes *should know how* (if such an expression may be used) to grow into distinct uteri." (emphasis added) What Darwin is asking is, "how do these cells know what to do, *for surely they can't think*." Cells thinking and making decisions would undercut random mutations and most certainly his idea of natural selection. This is one of the major shortfalls of early evolutionary theory that has carried on to this day. Again, according to the Darwinians, cells/organisms are passive recipients of Nature rather than active participants. So, it is *extra*-cellular events, prompted by Nature that are creating the alterations to coding sequences and directing the evolution of species by culling out the unfit and fine-tuning specific systems. It would seem that what we call science and scientific explanations are determined by an elite and what filters down to the non-academics is censored by these elites. There are many examples of information left out of explanations of, for example, cultural development. The use of mind-altering substances is one, and for art historians, teaching at prestigious universities, to miss all the mushrooms of the *Amanita muscaria* variety along with Psilocybin and cannabis in Christian art from 300 CE (Current Era) to the beginning of the twentieth- century is inexcusable (see Rush 2011 and 2013). How about "man-made global warming?" We are in an interglacial period and it is supposed to be warming up! You don't hear that on the news. So, which part is man-made? And then there is the metaphysics that glides by as science such as the universe came from nothing (see Krauss 2013), or the multi-verse (see Carroll 2019), and string theory (Kaku 2021). All these represent ideas, concepts, and opinion, not scientific fact, although they are promoted as strong possibilities. Darwin's concept of natural selection is another metaphysical concept passed off as science. Kaku, in his most recent work (2021), critically looks at the multi-verse, string theory, and so on, acknowledging there are problems connected to each. In terms of evolution of life forms he comments:

> Everywhere we look around us, we see objects of great complexity. But the sophistication of life-forms surrounding us can be explained by evolution. With enough time, pure chance can drive evolution via the survival of the fittest, so more sophisticated designs arise randomly from less sophisticated designs. A first designer for life is not necessary (2021: 187).

I am disappointed that Kaku can outline problems with numerous theories of cosmic origins but he appears content with random mutations and natural selection (a circular argument "outlawed" by science) as driving forces of evolution. There is no critical thinking in this matter. This is another example of how deeply entrenched – not unlike the belief in a god – Darwin's faith-based hypothesis has become even after decades of research that refutes the Darwinian position. From Harvard University to Berkeley we hear the same mantra, Random Mutations + Natural Selection + Time =

the Origins of Life and New Species. This is the protocol that students are instructed and expected to accept as fact, to give as feedback on exams acknowledging they have absorbed the "truth." After talking with a number of anthropologists it is obvious that few continue to believe in a *strict* interpretation of the Darwinism model, but what keeps it going is fear of retaliation, the fear of being shunned by one's peers (this is how small group leaders keep their flock in line). If Darwinism doesn't qualify as a faith-based tradition, a cult or religion in fact, I don't know what does. I have more to say about why this mantra continues to echo in the halls of academia in Chapter 8.

What is "Thinking?"

Mammals, birds, and other animals probably solve basic problems in a similar manner. Humans are not the apex of problem solvers; like all other animals, we are specialists. Problem solving involves "thinking" about a problem and the decisions or choices that follow, and, at the endocellular level, problems are complex and involve a thinking process very different from how you and I think. Endocellular thought processes have to take into consideration the status of every organ, every tissue, and probably every cell in the organism, a thought and decision-making process way beyond human capability, even using supercomputers. Decisions are more likely solved at the quantum level because it is within this arena that all can be computed at once, unlike modern day computers that solve problems incrementally, digitally, with 0 and 1. At the quantum level 0 and 1 can be computed at the same instant (McFadden and Al-Khalili 2014: 102). This is more analog, like the clock on the kitchen wall where you see the hands and all the numbers at once, along with the wall, color of the wall, perhaps the refrigerator, chairs, toaster, coffee maker, the cat, your mate, perhaps your mother-in-law, and so on. When you look at the clock you see everything within that frame; you compute it all at once but you leave out all that is irrelevant. This is what some scientists believe is going on at the quantum level, where in a fraction, of a fraction, of a fraction of a second the problem is computed, along with deleting the irrelevant information and noise, and a decision is rendered, for example, "time to go to work." If we understood computation at this level, and could apply it, we could produce, from scratch, any living lifeform. As Richard Feynman is reported to have said, "What I cannot create, I do not understand." Well, a living, functioning cell *does* understand itself and *can* recreate itself. A cell has to understand itself right down to the quantum level. We need to show a little respect. We humans do not adequately understand, at least at the conscious level, the codes for building life; compared to the cell, we are grossly ignorant. You see, there is a part of us that is very, very smart, but the conscious "us" isn't smart enough to figure it out – maybe in time. This really is a dilemma; a part of you is immensely smarter than the ego "you."

Moreover, what is trying to survive is not any particular test of the code of life. In short, it isn't all about us; it is about sustaining life and cellular adaptation to changing circumstances or slowing down entropy.

Consciousness and Awareness

Consciousness has been defined in many ways; lots of books on the subject. When I was studying medical hypnosis those many years ago I was told that the word "consciousness" is neutral and, like a lightbulb, it is either on (awake) or off (not awake). What is important is *awareness*. Awareness alters from moment to moment depending on the situation; stress alters awareness, as does relaxation. For example, when you are watching TV you experience one type of awareness; when someone knocks on your door you experience another, and so on. All living things are in their own way aware of their surroundings. Awareness is a method for the cell to monitor stress and stressors, in short, to monitor Nature. The subconscious, and its levels of awareness, is the provenience of dreams, deep meditation, and hypnosis. I will have more to say about dreams in Chapter 6.

Problem solving involves collecting sufficient information in order to make informed decisions. For cells to make proper decisions they need internal (with certain information likely coming from the quantum realm – more on the quantum realm in Chapter 6) as well as external information input. This information comes through your senses and, importantly, reactions to specific stressors (heat, cold, nutritional, predator), especially those that are interpreted as a threat to life and limb. Why do you think most of us often pick out the negative in the world before the positive? Wandering the Serengeti, and admiring the landscape – some flowers, the clouds perhaps, the mountain in the distance, a lizard scurrying across a rock, but missing the lion hiding by the bush carries little survival potential. The point. Mechanisms that contribute to new species are complex and, in my opinion, involve awareness of environmental processes, alerting the "inner self" of necessary changes, either immediately or for the next generation. With long periods of regular, for example, seasonal changes the cell can easily alter its coding in anticipation of these changes – and perhaps those that are less frequent but more devastating. Catastrophic events are a challenge and *if the right alterations occur during the minor fluctuations, these could lead to preadaptations.* The question for Darwinians is, where do the preadaptations come from? Is this simply the accumulation of random mutations? Random events don't create codes, let alone preadaptations to anything. The cellular communication interface with awareness of the external circumstances, allowing the cell/ organism to alter its DNA, would seem to be a *necessary* survival mechanism. Life has to stay ahead of Nature or perish. Life is smart.

CHAPTER 3

More on Natural Selection

RECALL the definition of natural selection offered in Chapter 1, that is, it is based on reproductive success. This, however, is meaningless which was even suspected by Darwin. I have goldfish swimming in one of the ponds on the property. Herons love fish, which make up most of their diet. At least once each summer a heron will be looking down at the pond, and when it sees a fish it swoops down – lunch. The bird can't get them all; the one that's eaten is the one it sees. Does this make these others, perhaps seven or eight, more fit, or just luckier?

According to Darwin, Nature culls out the unfit (perhaps the goldfish should have been looking up!) with the organism being a passive recipient of what Nature throws at it. In other words, Nature is in charge of evolution and the cell has little or no say.

Natural selection is actually wrapped around death and who leaves behind the most information that is then carried to the next generation and beyond. So, the most fit is a numbers game. If I sire 20 children that would make me more fit than the guy who only sires 2 or 3. So, the most fit is the male who has the most productive (no birth control) sex? The same thing, however, does not apply to women; pregnancy is dangerous. Women can't spread their genes all over the place, so how do we measure fitness between males and females of the species? Reproduction is a matter of getting coding sequences to the next generation *not specific* coding sequences. Nature cannot select for brawn or brain, skin color, hair color – it can only select for coding sequences (all or none) that make it (or don't make it) to the next generation. That, then, is our first problem with natural selection. This is a random process and Nature selects across the board, so to speak; there is no specificity or fine-tuning. Nature selects the luckiest.

Darwin oversold his concept of natural selection using a great deal of anecdotal information on bugs, birds, and such, and he plainly had doubts. Talking about what geneticists called "junk genes" in the 1970s, he states (2019: 59):

> . . . [In] the earlier editions of my "Origin of Species" *I perhaps attributed too much to the action of natural selection or the survival of the fittest. I have altered the fifth edition of the 'Origin' so as to confine my remarks to adaptive changes of structure*; but I am convinced, from the light gained during the last few years, that *very many structures which now appear to us useless, will hereafter be proved to be useful, and will therefore come within the range of natural selection*. (emphasis mine)

Let's consider what Darwin has written. First, he believes he has over stated his case and attempts to redefine fitness as "adaptive changes of structure." How do you define "adaptive," because natural selection isn't specific? It would seem we are back to what survives is adaptive (or it wouldn't survive), so those who survive with those traits are the most adaptive. We're back to a circular argument again. What he seems to mean is alterations to the phenotypes, for example, length of legs, a different shaped tooth, and so on. Now we are into epigenetics, *endocellular selection*, and the *cell's* alteration of phenotypes because Nature is not specific; Nature doesn't choose the good, the bad, and the ugly. She just *blindly* selects. If Nature has a purpose the Darwinians need to rethink all this because that smacks of intelligence. They can't have it both ways.

Second, how do these useless structures he mentions get turned back on when they are needed? They already exist, but are dormant, so how do they get selected, again, when they are needed? They don't work, and, without the cell turning these genes back on (epigenetics), how would they ever, specifically, be selected? How is this random? This has to be an inhouse issue, that is, the cell making choices. If the reader can agree on this point then you might also have to agree that the cell or organism can turn on and off other forms of information leading to phenotypic differences and new species.

He goes on to say (Darwin 2019: 59-60) "natural selection has been the chief agent of change, though largely aided by the inherited effects of habit, and slightly by the direct action of the surrounding conditions." This sounds strangely Lamarckian. The way out, of course, is to say the "inherited effects of habit" are the product of natural selection. Yes, you can produce a lot of offspring hoping that some will survive. But, those that do survive through luck may not be "fit" in terms of survival under prevailing conditions or in the future. The goldfish plucked from the pond might have been the biggest, strongest, most virile of the lot. The rest, not so much, so the fittest, then, are the "not so much."

Regardless of reproductive success, catastrophic events can wipe out whole species which can lead to totally new plants and animals. Those most fit, then, would be defined as those that survive the catastrophe, members of which supposedly had preadaptations in place that lead to the new species. "Fitness" is a slippery concept as reproductive success may have little or nothing to do with these animals that survive, and preadaptations may not be randomly created.

There is really no way of knowing what traits have the highest survival value – *unless you can predict the future*. We humans would like to believe it is our brand of intelligence that makes us most fit. This might be true. We are aware of the limitations of planet Earth as a permanent home. And just like an apartment or tenement structure it won't last forever, it is torn down, and replaced. Planet Earth is no different as we keep our eye on the sky for dangerous, near Earth objects. Soothsayers have been predicting the end of the world for thousands of years, perhaps from stories handed down of real catastrophic events of the past, and it will happen. Global warming is the least of our problems, and, as global warming is part of a cycle, we likely can't do anything about it (we can certainly do something about pollution). Our thinking ahead on these issues has survival potential, just as the cell's ability to think ahead has great survival value.

Darwin states (2019:48): "Beneficial variations of all kinds will thus, either occasionally or habitually, have been preserved and injurious ones eliminated." How do we define *beneficial*? It would seem, because it is the fittest that survive, then those that survive have the "beneficial" changes. Again, we are back to that circular argument. Without being able to predict the future there is no way of knowing what is or isn't beneficial.

We have also learned that "mutation" rates change over time, although, if we are dealing with only random events, inter-species rates of change should be equal. According to ScienceDaily (https://www. sciencedaily.com/releases/2019/01/190122114851.htm):

> Over the past million years or so, the human mutation rate has been slowing down so that significantly fewer new mutations now occur in humans per year than in our closest primate relatives. This is the conclusion of researchers from Aarhus University, Denmark, and Copenhagen Zoo in a new study in which they have found new mutations in chimpanzees, gorillas and orangutans, and compared these with corresponding studies in humans.

Why have human alterations in coding sequence rates gone down over the past million or so years? Mutations are variations, and the "mutations" noted by the researchers may be endocellular. One way to confirm this is to look at the fine-tuning of systems. The human body is built on a platform, a generic that appeared over 400 MYA in the Ordovician Period, and has been modified many times since then. In our (*Homo sapiens*) present generic configuration for over two million years, the greatest change has been in the enlargement of the cerebral cortex. Perhaps brain power and information storage, for predicting the future, are the ultimate survival strategies, and mutation rates have slowed because there is very little to change – from the neck down. If that is the case, how is natural selection choosing which group of animals to alter or not alter? Is there an intelligence behind natural selection?

Nature is only the messenger; Nature does not instruct how to change or evolve. This change potential, in response to the messages of Nature, has to derive from within the cell, from within the organism. We may have reached a point, like cats and sharks, where very little improvement is necessary. If Nature is only a messenger without a boss, then endocellular selection or "directed mutations" have to be in play in order to specifically move toward intelligence as a survival strategy. Remember, what is trying to survive are the coding sequences and the information *at* the quantum level that informs the coding sequences.

The awareness of an organism represents the "eyes and ears," so to speak, of evolution. This information first collected by awareness and the mind, is then transmitted to the cell, which is then transferred to the quantum level. The quantum level then provides feedback, possibly providing outcomes, or what to change, to the cell proper. Cells *can't* predict the future, only anticipate from past experience (collected at the quantum level and derelict coding sequences). In a similar fashion, humans can't predict the future, but we can anticipate (where do you suppose this talent came from?). Some of this anticipation may come from what we call "intuition" or "gut" feeling. Intuition has at least two sources, first, one's own thoughts and beliefs, which are sometimes right, and, second, from deep within (almost always right), which may be the cell giving you feedback from the quantum level – messages from the ancestors, perhaps? This, of course, is metaphysics.

Natural Selection, Endocellular Selection, and Survival Potential
I have a far higher probability of survival in any environment, under any circumstance, if I can predict and adapt. Being able to

predict and alter behavior, in short, staying ahead of Nature and having some control over my future, increases survivability into that future.

Natural selection does not plan for the future; natural selection does not play chess with life, "If I move my pawn, then X, then Y, then . . ." But life may play chess with Nature. Life stockpiles experiences, most likely in the form of derelict coding sequences (once called "junk genes") as well as at the quantum level, and it is through experience we solve problems. Take a look around. What do you have that protects you from Nature? Your house, your shoes, your condoms, on and on. We have these "things" because of the experiences of our ancestors who, instead of quivering under a bush, built shelters and, perhaps more importantly through language, constructed stories that helped to explain the give and take of Nature and how to predict and alter future outcomes. Fortunetellers and oracles have been around for thousands and thousands of years. Why do you suppose people read their horoscopes, or go to tarot readers and other soothsayers? We, deep down, want control over our future which means controlling or at least protecting self and others from heat, cold, wild animals, starvation, and so on, all of which are current and *future* concerns. This is a survival mechanism deeply imbedded in life, that is, right down into the quantum level. The cell's abilities, through communication and decision making, allows it to alter its destiny. Life is in a continual battle against Nature (death, entropy), although we are part of that Nature, and life would not exist if it didn't have a say in its future existence.

Natural selection sounds good, it sounds reasonable, but the most fit are only defined as the ones that survive. If Nature is truly selective, then there would have to be some energy behind natural selection directing life forms to some absolute fitness. Some researchers, Darwin included, believe intelligence is that absolute form of fitness, and it may be. And, of course, the Anglo-Saxons are the most intelligent of all, just look what they have accomplished as opposed to the "savages" who inhabit most of the world! This ethnocentric, or rather "elite-centric" prejudicial attitude is very much alive in the world today.

In a word, if there is a single, testable, scientific process that undermines Darwin's concept of natural selection it is endocellular selection, or the cell's ability to alter a trait's expression by the addition and subtraction of chemicals from the DNA molecule and other alterations to coding sequences. Without cellular thinking and decision making, epigenetics, for example, would not occur. Methylation occurs at 70 to 80 percent of the CpG marks on animal DNA and recent research clearly indicates that it is the cell itself, the organism itself, that is adding or subtracting these units except in the rare case of a random mutation (i.e. UV radiation, carcinogens, etc.). *And, the epigenetic alterations obviously pass into the next generation or we would not see methylation on 70 to 80 percent of the CpG marks on coding sequences.* This is part of what I term *endocellular selection.* Cells alter their DNA in other ways, as explained in Chapter 1 and in the following pages, and what this tells us is that lifeforms are more involved in "selection" than was previously thought – or even considered.

Review

We are lulled into a false "truth" through Darwin's numerous anecdotal stories of insect appendages, coloring of feathers, cranial characteristics, and so on, but none of it supplies us with a definition of fitness, other than those that survive. For Darwin, however, the less fit, the vicious and ignorant are the ones who produce the most offspring, at least in stratified societies. Nature selects "fitness," but without a definition of what "fitness" is, all you are left with are anecdotes and unconscionable insensitivity toward those deemed "unfit." Fitness is not defined except as a random outcome.

Survival demands specificity, for example, the development or modification of a specific trait during, or in anticipation of changes in the environment. Natural selection does not include specificity. Moreover, all we have for natural selection *is* a definition, that is, the outcome of natural selection, in a word, "fitness." So, the definition of "fitness" is fitness. This is like saying the definition of "virus" is a virus, or a virus is a virus. There is no information here.

The politics that surrounds Darwinism is shameful. The big push for Darwin, and certainly those who bought into his narrative, was an attempt to undermine creationism with science. Creationism, and a literal translation of the Bible, held up our understanding of who we are and how we got here for hundreds of years. Heresy was not lightly considered by the Catholic Church and other Christian denominations who donated large sums of money to various academic institutions. After the acceptance of Darwin, the story changed, and political pressure was and is brought to bear to maintain a narrative known by scholars, in these very institutions, to be less than correct. The same is in play today; it is heresy to suggest Darwin is wrong, and to preach anything other than Darwinism is considered sacrilegious in the academic community. This amounts to academic censorship. One has to wonder how much academic censorship goes on? In more recent times, again, we have been presented, essentially, metaphysics as science in the multi-verse theory, string theory, and so on, and, presented by those considered "in authority" as some sort of "fact" rather than hypothesis and conjecture. In short, metaphysics becomes science if it serves the needs of those in authority.

Finally, it is largely thought that anyone contradicting Darwin must be promoting religion. Endocellular selection, epigenetics, symbiosis, and hybridization have nothing to do with religion, and, in light of what we now know about cellular communication, and the communication and exchange of information between different lifeforms, we need to move on.

Cultural Insensitivity

Darwin lived in a bubble of privilege and prestige which comes through many of his examples.

There is reason to believe that vaccination has preserved thousands, who from a weak constitution would formerly have succumbed to the small-pox. Thus the weak members of civilized societies propagate their kind. No one who has attended to the breeding of domestic animals will doubt that this must be highly injurious to the race of man. It is surprising how soon a want of care, or care wrongly directed, leads to the degeneration of a domestic race; but excepting in the case of man himself, hardly any one is so ignorant as to allow his worst animals to breed" (Darwin 2019: 125- 126).

He makes similar statements throughout his book. Darwin is making what he considers, I suppose, a good case for eugenics and racial cleansing. Google the eugenics movement in the US, and, of course, you all know the name, Adolph Hitler. How about the Muslim Turks (1915-1916) murdering 1.2 million Armenian Christians in their ethnic cleansing efforts? And then there was Lenin and Starlin. The list is long, of elites and their treatment of non-elites; this is disgraceful.

Darwin makes statements and then presents the other side allowing himself an out if criticized. "Natural selection acts only tentatively. Individuals and races may have acquired certain indisputable advantages, and yet have perished from failing in other characters" (Darwin 2019: 132). Is natural selection a driving force toward "fitness" or is it not? Read Darwin carefully; he presents an idea but then back peddles giving himself an exit. Darwin would have been a good politician.

Darwin and Sexism

I first encountered Darwin's works as an undergraduate in the early-1960s. Liberation movements were in full swing and I was struck by Darwin's attitude toward women.

Man is more courageous, pugnacious and energetic than woman, and has a more inventive genius (Darwin 2019: 525).

He even compared women to children using cranial features as his proof.

Male and female children resemble each other more closely than the mature male. The female, however, ultimately assumes certain distinctive characters, and in the formation of her skull, is said to be intermediate between child and the man (Darwin 2019: 526).

But Darwin's main thrust was intellectual ability.

The chief distinction in the intellectual powers of the two sexes is shown by man's attaining to a higher eminence, in whatever he takes up, than can woman – whether requiring deep thought, reason, or imagination, or merely the use of the senses and hands. If two lists were made of the most eminent men and women in poetry, painting, sculpture, music . . . history, science, and philosophy, with half-a-dozen names under each subject, the two lists would not bear a comparison. We may also infer, from the law of the deviation from averages, so well illustrated by Mr. Galton, in his work on 'Hereditary Genius,' that if men are capable of a decided pre-eminence over women in many subjects, the average of mental power in men must be above that of women (Darwin 2019: 532).

I'm not sure many women in the West would accept Darwin's logic. What Darwin also didn't know has to do with the fact that the human female has two X chromosomes, with one of the Xs, for the most part, turned off. (You might wonder how this was "turned off" because it must have been fully functional for the male prior to conception.) The male is stuck with a single X and a puny Y. If both the Xs were turned on in the female, as some have suggested, she would be Superwoman, with abilities "far beyond that of mortal man," to borrow a phrase. What Darwin also didn't appreciate is that *men are expendable*, women are not; no life comes into this world, no immortality, no "life everlasting" except through the female. Most men have forgotten this.

Darwin's position of slow, incremental changes leading to new species and natural selection are interspaced with raciest and sexist remarks that would not be acceptable in today's media. It appears the intellectuals are cutting Darwin a break seeing that these were common positions in Darwin's day. However, these same intellectuals do not allow the same latitude with it comes to the founders of this country. The reasons for this can only be understood from a political standpoint, not from a scientific perspective. This is most unfortunate in that the politics wrapped around Darwinism, just as in the case of religion, has stood in the way of our understanding of who we are and where we came from. Darwinism became a religion based on faith, faith that Darwin's observations would eventually, scientifically prove correct – this has not happened and it's unlikely they ever will.

Fitness

The fittest creatures on the planet are viruses and bacteria, the *generics*, and above that all animals are fit and represent prototypes to see what is needed for survival under all conditions. Numbers of offspring isn't as important as survival strategies, biological and social. If all animals above bacteria and viruses are tests, what we have is an information system that accumulates coding sequences for new proteins over long periods of time. Life has to collect and store experiences as a means of anticipating Nature.

If numbers of offspring equal fitness, then there is no specific selection for intelligence, strength, etc., only survivors. As an example, one might consider intelligence, of the nature possessed by humans, the ultimate survival mechanism. But our type of intelligence may have little to do with numbers of offspring produced.

The domesticated house cat can begin producing offspring at about six months of age, can have ideally five litters a year, with each litter ranging from two to eight kittens. That is a lot of cats, but cats have sacrificed intelligence, of the type found in primates, in favor of stealth, night vision, and all kinds of sensory equipment. Cats are perfect predators; they have all that is required to obtain enough calories to reproduce and they don't need a large brain – it's all about food and sex.

Most feral house cats (*Felis catus*) living in the wild don't survive long after birth but those that do survive, is it because of numbers or are their other factors in play? The cat is designed with a nervous system perfectly matched to the carnivorous lifestyle, and, like sharks and alligators, has changed very little over immense periods of time – 20 million years for the cat (see Rush 2021). If random mutations can't produce codes and natural selection is only a numbers game and doesn't chose specific traits, where did all the fine-tuning come from, the stealth, the night vision, all the sensory organs, and so on? Answer: From the organism itself.

Darwinian evolution via natural selection selects for *preadaptations*, i.e. the organism already possessed the coding sequences making it more "fit." Where did these preadaptations come from, random mutations or directed mutations and endocellular selection?

So, we have many problems with Darwinian evolution, a major one being thought, decision making, and alterations of the coding sequences going on at the cellular level. Also, there is a problem with the word "fit" as it becomes a slippery value judgement. The ones that survive are the most fit and it's the most fit that survive. I don't think you can get more circular than that. If we include the cell, the organism, as an active participant in its evolution we avoid the value judgement and offer a more scientific explanation for the origin of species.

Individual Traits and Fine-Tuning

Natural selection, contrary to the population geneticists, does not select for individual traits, for example, intelligence. Again, it is all or nothing, and, because selection is arbitrary, how does Nature select to fine-tune anything? Nature provides information to which the organism responds. This brings us back to that heretical question, is this a passive response or are organisms actively involved in their own evolution?

The randomness of natural selection is on par with random mutations. Because there is a lack of specificity, and random can't build codes, there is no substance to the Darwinian position, only faith that one day science will prove them correct. Endocellular selection goes a long way in explaining the potential for self-survival into the future and mechanisms of change. In this sense, Darwinism is quite hollow.

Why Don't Some Animals Change Over Long Periods of Time?

Evolution is supposed to be a slow, gradual, random process, under control of natural selection – random mutations and natural selection should affect *all* plants and animals indiscriminately. So, why so little change over long periods of time in cats, sharks, alligators, crocodiles, and a host of others? Again, natural selection should affect all; all plants and animals should be in a perpetual state of random change. The reality is, this is not the case. How do the Darwinians explain this? I guess the answer is, just like God, "Nature acts in strange ways."

How Do Random Mutations and Natural Selection Create Codes?

Again, Darwinians don't inform as to how random mutations can create codes, and they don't inform as to how natural selection can select out or leave in specific traits that lead to survival. Again, Nature selects by chance not choice. The word "selection," as in natural selection, *assumes* specificity but what gets selected is arbitrary and not specific. Nature doesn't select; it indiscriminately plucks. This is like going into a hardware store blindfolded and indiscriminately pulling things off shelves and throwing them into a cart. The "selection" part of natural selection is a misnomer; there is no selection going on as that requires specificity. So, the individuals that produce more offspring, or survive the catastrophe, are not necessarily fit – again, they are lucky.

Another issue ignored by the Darwinians is, in order for natural selection to be of any use in origin of species, there has to be information to select. For example, the functional, reproducing cell had to be available before any type of selection could occur. How did natural selection select for the original cell? How did natural selection select for something before it existed? Let's go a little deeper into this.

Redfield comments (2001: 634):

Do bacteria have genes for genetic exchange? The idea that the bacterial processes that cause genetic exchange exist because of natural selection for this process is shared by almost all microbiologists and population geneticists. However, *this assumption has been perpetuated by generations of biology, microbiology and genetics textbooks without ever being critically examined.* (emphasis mine)

This non-critical attitude is non-scientific and, again, troublesome. What Redfield is getting at in the rest of his article is natural selection can't have much to do with the earliest lifeforms on this planet. Bacteria and archaea are single cell organisms that are self-sufficient in terms of reproduction. Schindler (2018) points out that bacteria can exchange information through conjugation, but this is totally separate from reproduction through fissioning. So, sexual selection, in a Darwinian sense, is not an issue. Bacteria have to be in place before any selection can occur – where did the bacteria come from if random mutations can't build codes and natural/sexual selection can't take place? What we see here, however, is exchange of information between bacteria which can, as Schindler points out, lead to resistance to antibiotics. The idea that such resistance is caused by a random mutation, an accidental development, needs to be more critically examined.

Life Leaves Little to Chance
So, there is a will to life, an energy that pushes life along, and it is unlikely that life would simply and passively allow Nature, through Darwinian random mutation and natural selection, to bend and shape the coding sequences. Nature supplies the

information, that is all, and living cells have to decide what to do with the information, what alterations to make, if that is called for. Nature does not select anything in particular – the fit are the ones that survive; the survivors are the fittest. Of all the research accumulated over the past 50 years epigenetics and endocellular selection in general inform that cells, the organisms themselves, are more actively involved in their evolution than once thought. Without active involvement, in my opinion, no life forms, self-reproducing or otherwise, would exist. We live in a dualistic universe and where there is death (entropy) there is life, an active attempt to slow down entropy.

The Darwinians think epigenetics is an insignificant issue in the development of new species. As Dawkins comments (Dawkins and Wong 2017: 221-222):

> There is an extension to epigenetics which is more controversial. This is the idea that the pattern of gene use can be passed on to future generations: epigenetic inheritance. We are feted with stories of characteristics being passed on from parent to offspring, in a modern resurgence of the Lamarckian idea of a blacksmith passing on his strong muscles to his children. There seems to be something in the human psyche to which this disastrous concept appeals – disastrous because it would also mean the blacksmith's child inheriting his father's gammy leg, scarred face and political attitudes . . .

It is obvious from Dawkins' remark that he knows very little about epigenetics. How is it that *random mutations* get passed onto future generations but *changes the cell makes* cannot be passed on? In short, and according to Dawkins, the only changes that get passed on are the *random* changes, I guess because they are somehow more important, or maybe Nature "acts in strange ways?" Dawkins needs to clarify this.

Moreover, nowhere in modern research has any scientist suggested inheritance of a "scarred face" and "gammy leg." And, yes, the blacksmith will pass on his muscles to his children, and their ability to enlarge, and to what degree through exercise *may* be epigenetic, especially if blacksmithing carried on for several generations. Even Darwin suggested this, as mentioned earlier.

Some authors think that epigenetics reflects the Darwinian position. Meyer (2021: 209), for example, thinks epigenetics fails to offer much to understanding the history of life. In my opinion, Meyer is absolutely wrong. In fact, epigenetics undermines natural selection and tends to bolster his position of an intelligence behind life's development over time. Epigenetics is just one aspect of the origin of species, but what it doesn't tell us is where the original coding came from to build biological systems?

The Concept of the Generic

A generic is the base, the platform upon which everything that enhances the continuation of the generic is attached. Bacteria just show up on planet Earth around 3.5 BYA (Billion Years Ago), and they are likely extraterrestrial. This, of course, informs little as to origins or how life initially came about.

We have identified fossilized bacteria is ancient rock, or rock that has not been recycled through plate tectonics. Some of this rock, for example, can be found on the east coast of Canada and Northwestern Australia. Bacteria or prokaryotes (and there were several types found) are single cell animals that are irreducibly complex, for removal of any of the internal structures (e.g. ribosomes) would lead to cell death. These bacteria apparently fed on simple sugars (glucose, perhaps, a very stable sugar), or other organic substances, which theoretically were components of the "primordial soup" (see Thaxton 1986: 42-68 and improbability of life originating in the primordial soup). Organic compounds, by the way, are carbon compounds, like the bread you're eating or the coffee you're drinking.

The companion to the bacteria is the virus, most assuredly right there in the beginning, an antagonist, if you will, to take advantage of immortality, by developing symbiotic relationships of one intensity or another with bacteria. Think of the virus as an information source, an encyclopedia, that can be drawn upon when necessary. The virus and the bacteria are the generics but where did the coding for these lifeforms come from? I don't know, but the Darwinians think it a product of chance – I think this highly unlikely. How can you randomly mutate or select for something before it exists?

Bacteria, archaea, and viruses then, are the base line generics on this planet, but generics go beyond this and enter into irreducible complexity. For example, teeth, a generic, just show up. They may be connected to the horny, beak-like mouth of the Ordovician Nautiloid, Orthoceras (485-443 MYA) but there doesn't seem to be any intermediate forms (Rush 2021: 65-66). The tooth, becomes a generic, a platform, if you will, because, epigenetically this generic base line can take on many shapes and sizes. Teeth are extremely important for the paleontologist because a change in phenotype (for example, rounded cusps changed to cone or blade shape) informs us of a new food quest. Because we are altering the *expression* of the tooth this does not necessarily require altering the amino acids that make up the coding sequence(s).

The bipedal hominin body has likely been in place for seven or eight million years. Prior to this, and to get to us, the cells need to alter the characteristics of the skeletal structure. In other words, we have the generic beginning with fish, and after successive catastrophic events (major characteristics are altered possibly in the wave form) leading to amphibians, then reptiles, and mammals. In each case we are fine-tuning the generic. For hominins like us, there are, as in the forerunners, simultaneous alterations to several part of the skeletal structure creating a variation on the original generic, that is, bipedalism. For example, a locking out knee joint has to be in place before it can be fine-tuned. You need a foot designed for walking (not running), with the toes in alignment with the most medial toe, or hallux, which is much more robust, with the most lateral toe much reduced in size. An arch is not necessary but there needs to be a "ball" or padded area posterior to the hallux cushioning the metatarsals.

A generic foot would be something like Lucy's (*Australopithecus afarensis*, footprints dated to 3.4 MYA) and it can be fine-tuned epigenetically. We have curious footprints from Crete, dated to 5.7 MYA, highly suggestive that the generic foot, designed for walking, has been around much longer than originally considered (see Bohme 2020: 107-117).

The pelvis has to have assumed a bowl shape; the os coxa are lateral rather than dorsal as in a chimp. I think it highly probable that the bowl-shaped pelvis, locking out knee joint, and the generic foot show up at the same time. These three (at least) seem to go together as a unit; a foot made for walking requires a specific type of knee joint and pelvis. Randomly altering these structures independently seems unlikely and, because random doesn't come with intent, random can't possibly, accidently, alter all these structures at once. *Ardipithecus ramidus* is a good example where you have an improbable reconstructed pelvis matched with a chimp's feet! Those feet have no need for a locking out knee joint or bowl-shaped pelvis. What is the survival value of a human-like pelvis and chimp-like feet and hands? Ardi's feet and hands are designed for an off the ground, tree living environment; Ardi isn't spending much time on the ground. Also, Ardi doesn't need a bowl-shaped pelvis, locking out knee joint, or platform foot to move around on the ground. Just ask any chimp. In my opinion, the reconstruction of Ardi, and the interpretation given, are unlikely.

In my opinion, bipedalism is a specific alteration to the generic. We can see the possible presidents for it in orangutans but there does not seem to be a gradual change from orangutans to on-the-ground bipedalism. Our lineage diverged from the orangutans sometime between 18 and 14 MYA and it is possible that bipedalism shows up shortly after that time period. Around 15 MYA we start to see a slow and continual cooling which would indicate the need for acquiring new food sources and/or migration into warmer areas. In any case, conceivably there was no gradual change into bipedalism; the bowl-shaped pelvis, locking out knee joint, and platform foot just show up possibly after a drop in temperature (acute cold stress) during that point in the Miocene. Perhaps these gradations will be unearthed in the future. Again, I think it reasonable to suggest that the configuration of the pelvis, knee, and foot show up at the same time, and I think this time frame may be much earlier than 8 MYA. Bohem (2021) may be correct in her position that this generic (bipedalism – pelvis, knee, and foot) may first have appeared in Eurasia and not Africa.

Generics, like a tooth, just seem to show up and then are fine-tuned epigenetically over long periods of time. Most of the alterations to the phenotype are reactions to contemporary stressors, but there is always a mind to the future, to catastrophic occurrences and survival past such events. This is why new species just show up after major catastrophic events; the cell has thought ahead, it has preadapted itself.

CHAPTER 4

The Universe and Life as Self-Organizing

IN 1969, Kenyon and Steinman brought to light the idea that the universe and life within came about through chemical self-organization. Realizing that certain chemicals have an affinity for one another, for example, oxygen and numerous minerals (iron, copper, lead), they proposed that this affinity is what established the universe and life-forms. Kenyon later abandoned his original position realizing that there are many chemical situations where such affinity doesn't exist yet chemicals bond together. Kenyon (1986: vii) states:

> Finally, in this brief summary of the reasons for my growing doubts that life on earth could have begun spontaneously by purely chemical and physical means, there is the problem of the origin of genetic, i.e. *biologically relevant*, information in biopolymers. *No experimental system yet devised has provided the slightest clue as to how biologically meaningful sequences of subunits might have originated in prebiotic polynucleotides or polypeptides.* Evidence for some degree of spontaneous sequence ordering has been published, but there is no indication whatsoever that non-randomness is biologically significant. Until such evidence is forthcoming one certainly cannot claim that the possibility of a naturalistic origin of life has been demonstrated.

By non-randomness Kenyon is referring to spontaneous organization which would then have to proceed in a non-random fashion. This is important, and until the Darwinians have a scientific explanation for this they can't claim life and new species are created through random chance.

Kenyon (1986: viii) brings up a very significant point which has more to do with politics and an unwillingness to consider all possibilities even when they do not fit one's cherished beliefs.

If the authors' criticisms are valid, one might ask, why have they not been recognized or stressed by workers in the field? I suspect that part of the answer is that many scientists would hesitate to accept the authors' conclusion that it is fundamentally implausible that unassisted matter and energy organized themselves into living systems. Perhaps these scientists fear that acceptance of this conclusion would open the door to the possibility (or the necessity) of a supernatural origin of life. Faced with this prospect many investigators would prefer to continue in their search for a naturalistic explanation of the origin of life along the lines marked out over the last few decades, in spite of the many serious difficulties of which we are now aware. Perhaps the fallacy of scientism is more widespread than we like to think.

So, do we need to take a closer look at what passes for science? I think we do. From origin of species, to global warming, and the germ theory of disease we are not getting passing grades; we can do better than this. A great deal of what we call science has been taken over by the politic.

CHAPTER 5

Endocellular Selection

SO, if random mutations and natural selection (plucking) are not driving the origin of species, what is? The simple answer is, the cells, the organism itself. Even Richard Dawkins (2006: 29) admitted this when he stated genes are at least partially responsible for their own survival and therefore must play an active part in it; the informational coding sequences that run the show are not passive recipients of what Nature (environmental stressors outside the cell) throws at them. Biological evolution requires cellular communication and decision making or what I term *endocellular selection*. What evidence is there to support this heretical thesis?

Multicellular organisms signal using three general chemical types: autocrine (secretion of hormone that binds to autocrine receptors on the cell altering its behavior), paracrine (secretion of chemicals to induce changes in nearby cells altering their behavior), endocrine (hormonal cells placed in circulation to target cells at various distances), and through direct contact. I'm going to keep this very complex subject brief and simple. For those of you who desire detail and images see Chandar and Viselli 2019.

For you and me, we send signals visually, auditorily, and kinesthetically or through body language. We also respond to chemicals (through smell and taste), body odors, for example, including pheromones which are supposedly picked up subconsciously. What is of note, and I will go into this in some depth in Chapter 8, is that, for the human animal, pheromones change (both male and female) during pregnancy and after a child is born. Apparently male testosterone levels drop early during the pregnancy (see https://www.webmd.com/men/ news/20141217/expectant-dads-may-also-have-hormonal-changes study-suggests). Although not stated by the authors, male testosterone levels begin to "normalizes" shortly after parturition (if male and female are in close, daily contact) and certainly within 12-18 months. The importance of this, in terms of the alleged "pair bond" and male monogamy, will be discussed in Chapter 8.

The point here is the way we humans consciously communicate is not the same method of communicating at the cellular level; cells aren't using iPhones, no emails or love letters are sent or received. And it's hard to image the power certain chemicals/proteins have in sending and receiving information in order for living systems to function. Biological cells, for example, heart, lung, and kidney, are in instantaneous contact through chemical signals. The chemicals produced send specific messages to stimulate nutrient intake, toxin removal, warning of injury, microbial attack, and so on, and certain types of cells, for example, T cells, *can alter genetic coding*. This is a great deal of information to analyze, it has to happen quickly, and has, at least in part, to occur at the quantum level where, as mentioned, Os and 1s as waves, not particles, can be computed in a parallel fashion apparently instantly (see McFadden and Al-Khalili 2014).

Cells respond to external information (stressors) provided by Nature, that is, heat, cold, and so on, and we can see Nature as the messenger or: information –> senses – > cell –> quantum level –> cell and alteration of coding sequences. In my opinion, little happens until the quantum level gives feedback to the cell. The cell then acts. This occurs as fast as things can happen or Planck time which is 5.39×10^{-44} seconds (perhaps even faster at the quantum level if time is irrelevant), which represents the maximum number of events that can happen in a second. This is very, very quick, unimaginably quick, so quick that at the quantum level, somehow working with waves (maybe strings), every molecule in a cell, or a human being for that matter, perhaps even the universe can be "in touch" (instant email). With the feedback likewise comes a solution or solutions. What I think is difficult to grasp is the amount of cellular/quantum communication that goes on and how rapidly responses occur. I see this every day in our garden as we grow much of our food. A summer squash fruit can double or triple its size overnight. We grow giant sunflowers that, especially when it is hot, grow 6 to 8 inches in the course of a day. It's hard to imagine the number of molecules involved and information transfer that has to occur for that kind of growth. Many plants are seasonal and perennials often go dormant, so the plants don't have much time for growth and maturity. Humans are long lived, and time is less compressed for a slower growth rate. This is especially true for animals who have to learn a great deal to survive, for example, primates; much of the information has to do with social interaction and perhaps technological issues. Coding sequences that promote rapid or slow growth in plants might be useful during our journeys to other worlds, for speeding up plant growth, for example.

In any event, we are accustomed to things happening in seconds, minutes, hours, days, and so on. It appears, at the quantum level, everything happens at once. I remember seeing graffiti in a men's bathroom, Sidney Smith Hall, "Time was invented to keep everything from happening at once." This was over 50 years ago and I don't imagine the graffiti is still on the wall, but that is one of the issues here. This is why Einstein's General and Special Relativity don't fit the quantum world – time and space are not relevant, or in some manner they are merged in such a way as to cancel each other out. For us, without time and space, nothing can happen; I can't even conceive of a way to imagine existence without time and space. That is probably a key in all this; we can't imagine the quantum realm because it exists in another dimension with a different set of rules. Dreaming, along with deep meditation and hypnosis, however, might be exceptions; more about this later.

It's important to keep in mind that Nature is neutral; Nature is information to which cells and the organisms of which they are composed respond. In this sense, Nature doesn't select; *it only provides opportunity.* Nature providing opportunity is a key factor in the origin of species. Alterations in climate and catastrophic events provide new prospects, new codes for what works and what doesn't.

Epigenetics

Originally epigenetics referred to the addition or subtraction of methyl units (chemicals) from the base cytosine (the most unstable of the nucleotides that make up the DNA molecule), and the addition or subtraction of methyl, acetyl, and phosphorous units from histones around which the DNA molecule is wrapped 1.6 times. We now know that alterations to coding sequences goes way beyond this. I call this endocellular selection which includes epigenetics as well as all the other alterations the cell can accomplish.

Epigenetics, in part, is about the chemical attachments to DNA (specifically to the nucleotide cytosine), and the chemicals that adhere to the lysine tails of the histones, altering the expression of an animal's phenotype (that which is expressed, i.e. skin, hair, length of legs, size and shape of teeth, etc.). These chemicals are *additions* to or *subtractions* from the DNA code, the genotype (what is coded on the genes). Again, there is more to epigenetics than this. When these modifications happen randomly, these important chemicals are removed (I haven't found any literature that indicates random mutations add methyl units, etc.), and this can lead to disease. Random mutations remove information and this will have consequences for the rest of the structure. Epigenetics is one method, through cellular communication and decision making, by which *a cell can alter its DNA*, and when that occurs it doesn't qualify as random, it is purposeful. Remember, Nature, or the environment, only supplies information to which the cell responds, and there are many possibilities. Also keep in mind, that when random mutations occur the Darwinians allow these alterations to pass into the next generation; this, of course, is their method of creating new species. When it comes to changes the cell makes, there is great hesitation to allow these alterations to cross over, as we saw with Dawkins statement above. It seems that a different set of rules apply.

Epigenetic modifications are not incidental or occasional. According to Li and Zang (2014) methylation occurs at 70 to 80 percent of all CpG sites or marks, indicating the importance of methylation and changes in the expression of coding sequences. The chemical additions and subtractions alter the expression of the coding sequences, for example, making legs longer or shorter, adding more or less melanin in the skin, adding an extra set of fingers and toes, and so on. Also, many of these chemical additions and subtractions are already in place at conception and are modified during gestation, where the fetus is reacting to various types of stressors, that is, lack of nutrition in the mother, cold and heat stress, fear reactions from the mother, and so on. It is as if the fetus is planning for the future. These alterations just can't happen in one, just one, for example, human; this has to occur on the same coding sequences of many individuals at the same time before it is likely to be passed on to the next generation. Individuals in a group experiencing the same stressors are likely to alter the same coding sequences; we see this in rats (Marchlewicz et al. 2020: 7).

Organisms are not simply at the mercy of the environment as suggested by Charles Darwin and his followers. All lifeforms are active participants in their evolution with the key words, *endocellular communication* and external *stress*. As Lieff (2020: 1) states:

> The greatest secret of modern biological science, hiding in plain sight, is that all of life's activity occurs because of conversations between cells. During infections, immune T cells tell brain cells that we should "feel sick" and lie down. Long-distance signals direct white blood cells at every step of their long journey to an infection. Cancer cells warn their community about immune and microbe attacks. Gut cells talk with microbes to determine who are friends and enemies. Instructor cells in the thymus teach T cells not to destroy human tissues.

This key to modern medical science is hidden because it is impossible for most of us to understand the best current technical journals in neuroscience, genetics, molecular biology, immunology, and microbiology.

Much of the data regarding cellular communication comes from medical research asking specific questions, for example, how do cancer cells hijack other cells to do their bidding? Or, with Alzheimer's disease, why unfolded proteins are not removed from CSF (Cerebral Spinal Fluid) leading to "plaque" buildup affecting memory? Learning how cells communicate with other cells leads to a better understanding of the disease process and possible cures, as well as giving insights into the origin of species.

The study of cell communication focuses on how a cell gives and receives messages with its environment and with itself. Indeed, cells do not live in isolation. Their survival depends on receiving and processing information from the outside environment, whether that information pertains to the availability of nutrients, changes in temperature, variations in light levels, and predators. Cells can also communicate directly with one another — and change their own internal workings in response — by way of a variety of chemical and mechanical signals. In multicellular organisms, cell signaling allows for specialization of groups of cells. Multiple cell types can then join together to form tissues such as muscle, blood, and brain tissue. In single-celled organisms, signaling allows populations of cells to coordinate with one another and work like a team to accomplish tasks no single cell could carry out on its own (Neitzel and Rasband https://www.nature.com/scitable/topic/cell-communication-1412 2659/).

One of the most famous studies in epigenetics and cellular communication is the Dutch Hunger study which demonstrates that the fetus, during gestation, is planning for caloric/nutritional needs after parturition (see Rush 2020: 54, 62, 66) and thus altering its genetic coding and passing it on to the next generation. It is difficult to understand how this could happen randomly and the part natural selection played. Nature is not making decisions for the fetus; Nature is *information* and the fetus is altering itself relative to that information. And, in the case of those mothers suffering from starvation during the first trimester in the Dutch Hunger studies, children were born with the right birth weight but tended toward obesity as they got older usually developing diabetes. The fetus, apparently, was planning for a low caloric environment after birth, that is, food sources would be scarce. As astonishing as this is, the Dutch Hunger study is not a singular analysis. For example, recent research indicates, "[A]lthough DNA sequence is fairly permanent, epigenetic modifications are dynamic throughout the life course and can be heavily influenced by external factors such as environment and nutrition" (Marchlewicz, et. al. 2020: 4). The point is these additions and subtraction from DNA and histones are by no means unusual or trivial. But, epigenetics likewise affects other proteins and RNA sequences.

> In addition to DNA methylation, epigenetic regulation can control gene expression by proteins and RNAs that influence the accessibility of transcriptional machinery, known as *trans-epigenetics*. . . Histone modifications can determine the accessibility of the associated DNA to transcriptional machinery and influence gene expression in various biological conditions, development, and tumorigenesis (Chen et al. 2020: 286-287).

It would seem that limiting the role of epigenetics to chemical attachment to the DNA and histones, as indicated above, is premature as their effects range far and wide.

Much of the recent research into epigenetics has centered on diet and the alterations in coding sequences apparently to compensate for dietary deficiencies leading to various disease states. There has to be a "taking from Peter to give to Paul" in some priority manner, for the goal of life is to keep it going and a disease state, for example diabetes, is better than death. Keep in mind that malnutrition is only one type of stress that affects chemical additions or subtractions. Poor nutrition, however, appears to be one of the major issues in disease. The medical community has paid little attention to nutrition in the past and most medical doctors know very little about nutritional needs and prefer, forced by their protocols to prescribe drugs for heart problems, drugs and surgery for type-2 diabetes, and so on. As an aside, gastro-intestinal bypass, a very dangerous procedure, is bound to lead to malnutrition. A much easier solution is to shut off the person's taste buds for six months; I guarantee the patient will lose weight (there are some anti-fungal drugs that can accomplish this and it isn't permanent).

The medical community, as mentioned, has paid little attention to diet mainly because they assumed all the nutrients you need can be obtained from the food you eat, and, perhaps more importantly, a lack of interest in preventing disease. The USDA hasn't helped in this manner either with their graphs a reflection of what we eat culturally rather than what the individual needs. Obesity is a case in point.

Obesity risk appears to be perpetuated across generations by way of programmed DNA alterations that occur in utero and that affects gene expression throughout the life span.

Studies have demonstrated associations of maternal obesity and epigenetic changes, such as DNA methylation, histone modification, and chromatin remodeling, linked to adipose tissue growth and chronic disease risk in offspring. Diet has emerged as important in this regard, affecting epigenetic pathways in adipocytes (Claycombe et al. 2020: 323).

Staying with obesity for the moment, the thinking is, if the person is obese, then that person is well fed. This is definitely not the case, for consuming empty carbohydrates (mainly sugar and starch) means that essential amino acids, vitamins, minerals, and other phytochemicals may be in short supply. The body needs these substances without which the body moves toward disease, and, for the next generation "starvation genes" can be brought into play. In a word, we are addicted to the chemicals provided in fruits, vegetables, tubers, and the like, without which we experience ill health.

Clinical studies have shown that maternal protein-calorie malnutrition can contribute to the development of child obesity. . . This involves intrauterine undernutrition, which results in intrauterine growth restriction (IUGR) as well as epigenetic programming the offspring for survival in a nutrient poor postnatal environment. Such effects typically also involve accelerated postnatal "catch-up" growth and consequential development of obesity . . . and type-2 diabetes (T2D) in later life (Claycombe et al. 2020: 326).

But type-2 diabetes may also (in combination with other factors) be an unforeseen result of our shutting down the coding for uricase, mentioned in the Preface, the enzyme most mammals, including monkeys, utilize for removing uric acid from the blood. For humans and other apes, we excrete it through our kidneys as urine. As Johnson and Andrews comment (2011):

In the Middle Miocene (approximately 17 to 12 Ma) at least two radiations of fossil apes from East Africa into Eurasia occurred, and, while controversial, some paleoanthropological studies suggest that one of the Eurasian lineages may have returned to Africa to evolve into humans and the African apes. Here, we present a novel argument supporting this hypothesis. Specifically, the global cooling that occurred in the middle Miocene rendered hominoids living in Europe at risk for starvation as seasonal climate change resulted in less availability of fruits during the winter months. During this time, a mutation in uricase occurred in early hominids that resulted in a rise in serum uric acid. Uric acid has been found to potentiate the effect of fructose to increase fat stores, suggesting that the mutation provided a survival advantage. Such a survival advantage would have been less likely to occur in Africa, where the continued presence of tropical rainforests would have been more likely to provide food throughout the year. Furthermore, Miocene apes in Europe were in protected sites where geographic isolation could have allowed the uricase mutation to be rapidly expressed in the entire population. While speculative, we suggest that the uricase mutation supports an extra-Africa origin of humans.

So, epigenetic alterations and endocellular selection of coding sequences that occurred many millions of years ago, in reaction to some stressor (in the above case, seasonal lack of fruit/calories), turns out to be a problem in modern society. The loss of uricase in humans, however, has other consequence related to health, from negative (high blood pressure, gout, etc.) to positive, aiding in preventing neurodegenerative diseases (see Alvarez-Lario and Macarron-Vivcente 2015). I recall as an undergraduate reading a text in biochemistry that uric acid shares a similar chemical structure with caffeine, a known psychic energizer. Uric acid, then, might actually contribute to our intelligence.

The DOHaD [Developmental Origins of Health and Disease] hypothesis suggests that fetal programming is likely playing a role in the alarming increase in obesity of children and adolescents and will result in increased diabetes, increase in obesity of children and adolescents and will result in increased diabetes, cardiovascular disease, and early death during adulthood. . . (Farter et al. 2020: 53).

What I find both interesting and curious is these "mutations" show up exactly when needed those many millions of years ago. In today's world, however, storing too many carbohydrates leads to obesity, and, along with malnutrition, leads to type-2 diabetes. What we are seeing, in the ape genome, are modifications originally designed to help stave off starvation, especially when pregnant, that is, the storage of fat tissue during most of the year to tide them over the lean months. Life can think ahead, anticipate, but is not always able to foresee the effects, for example, of future cultural behaviors on caloric intake. Research into epigenetics also suggests that most nutritional issues can be prevented or reversed.

Cellular Toxicity and Alterations in Coding Sequences
Another issue that usually accompanies malnutrition is cellular toxicity which can contribute to altering coding sequences leading to disease states, such as cancer. Tobacco smoke is a major contributor to cellular toxicity leading to a high probability of lung cancer and failure in other organs. This is one of the reasons that second-hand smoke is dangerous; the toxins in tobacco smoke don't just stay with the smoker. Most cancers can be connected to epigenetic alterations (removal of methyl unites thus turning on coding sequences); inhaled tobacco smoke promotes cellular toxicity. Almost half the deaths each year in the US (2.5 million people die in the US each year) can be attributed to the use of tobacco over long periods of time. This doesn't seem to be much of an issue for the medical community (they kill around 15 percent of the 2.5 million with pharmaceutical drugs and botched operations), or our government, seeing the tobacco companies are still in business. You see, you don't need a gun to kill people. All you need to do is hand them a pack of cigarettes.

Constipation slows down toxin removal and most likely leads to many disease states, for example, high blood pressure, diverticulosis and likely diverticulitis, and so on. Constipation is usually caused by lack of fiber and water in one's diet. As stated by Van Gilder and Remington in STAT (January 19, 2017):

> Traditional medical education may include a token course in prevention, but the focus is squarely on how to treat patients. Once in practice, most physicians apply their expertise and time to immediate health problems. They don't know, and often feel they can't influence, whether their patients eat a healthy school lunch or have a safe place to ride a bike. At most, they often issue rote reminders to quit smoking or to lose a few pounds.

A similar situation obtains for the study of evolution, where an elite group continues to promote a system, Darwinism, which is clearly inadequate for explaining origins of species let alone the origin(s) of life. For academics in the biological sciences to promote Darwinism as truth and the only mechanism for the origin of species, are, to put it bluntly, lying to their students.

I want to remind the reader that stress related decisions made at the cellular level appear to plan for the future, but cells can make mistakes as noted – epigenetics/endocellular selection isn't all positive.

Although it is valuable to determine specific epigenetic modifications governing the regulation of fetal development, it is more imperative to clarify how these changes contribute to the overall health of the offspring. The activation of mammalian *AAR [Amino Acid Response] may act as a cue for the fetus to develop an adaptive response suited to its predicted postnasal environment but could in turn increase their vulnerability to developing disease and also influence their responsiveness to therapy.* A clear understanding of the molecular mechanisms at the epigenetic level for inflammatory genes will provide novel knowledge that is critical for preventing and/or treating a variety of inflammatory gene-related pathological conditions through epigenetic therapies (Pan et al. 2020: 99). (emphasis mine)

Stress is the major factor in epigenetic alterations and can come from many sources, many culturally derived. As I tell my students, culture can make you sick.

Perinatal exposure to methyl donor nutrients, protein restriction, dietary lipid, and total caloric intake impact DNA methylation, DNMT [DNA methyltransferase] activity, histone tail modifications, and miRNA [micro RNA] expressions (Marchlewicz et al. 2020: 29).

Coding sequences do not act alone and are mediated by numerous enzymes that assist in altering other coding sequences.

But these enzymes and other co-factors can't function properly without adequate nutrition. Although there are generalizations, each individual is different, responds uniquely to different foods and nutrients, and using a minimal requirement standard (USDA) is just that, minimal. Blood tests that reflect a standard deviation, for example, the average amount of B12, can likewise be misleading as *your* body may be designed to best function at the high (or low) end of that standard.

Quantum Tunneling and Cellular Communication

As pointed out above cellular communication is intense, and part of that communication requires, or is involved in altering coding sequences in order to adapt to prevailing circumstances. Studies in nutrition are hopefully catching the eyes and ears of the medical community, the message being prevention is easier than cure.

Getting back to cellular communication, some researchers suggest that it is enzymes that communicate with the quantum level, knitting the two realms together. This apparently occurs through quantum tunneling.

> . . . So, the discovery that some, and possibly all, enzymes work by promoting the dematerialization of particles from one point in space and their instantaneous materialization in another provides us with a novel insight into the mystery of life. And while there remain many unresolved issues related to enzymes that need to be better understood, such as the role of protein motions, there is no doubt that quantum tunneling plays a role in the way they work (McFadden and Al-Khalili 2014: 97).

More on enzymes, quantum tunneling, and endocellular communication shortly and in Chapter 6. For now, let's consider epigenetics and cellular communication in more detail.

> Epigenetics is defined as the study of heritable changes in gene expression without underlying changes in DNA sequence... DNA methylation and posttranslational modifications of histones are

good examples for epigenetic mechanisms that can regulate gene expression. Chromatin modifiers that mediate the methylation, acetylation, and other modifications of histones represents targets to elicit changes in gene expression. The activities of chromatin- modifying enzymes are regulated, in part, by the concentration of intermediary metabolites that are utilized as substrates or cofactors for enzymatic activity.

. . . Fortunately, many epigenetic modifications are reversible, leaving the door open for manipulation of chromatin-modifying enzymes through the consumption of bioactive food components as well as pharmacological agents (Pham and Lee 2020: 361).

Epigenetic Reaction to Stress

Stress comes in many forms, for example, nutrition discussed above, exposure to toxins, UV radiation, cold, parasites, emotional stress (fear, anxiety, etc.), physical injury, and so on. Epigenetic reactions to these stressors are seen across the animal kingdom.

Behavior- and stress-induced effects on the developing and adult epigenome are widespread from insects to mammals. For example, the desert locust (*Schistocerca gregaria*) produces more offspring of the gregarious swarming phenotype when bred in crowded conditions. . . Similarly, rats show persistent DNA methylation changes of the glucocorticoid receptor and many other gene loci in the hippocampus in response to high versus low levels of maternal care in the first week of life . . . Adult humans abused in early life display increased DNA methylation at the *NR3C1* glucocorticoid receptor promoter in the hippocampus . . .After being near cats, rats exhibit symptoms of posttraumatic stress syndrome concomitant with increased methylation in the *Bdnf* gene in the hippocampus. . . and increased methylation of this same gene is seen in human suicide victims. . . In mice, stress from maternal separation results in depressive behavior coupled with both increased and decreased DNA methylation in a number of genes. . . Interestingly, *these mice can transmit the DNA methylation pattern and phenotype transgenerationally through the male line . . .* Finally, early life stress in humans is also linked with gene expression changes for a polymorphic form of serotonin receptor. . . (Marchlewicz et al. 2020: 7). (emphasis added)

What we are realizing is a complexity that can't possibly be random, and coding, written into cell development and maintenance, that can't be selected for naturally to the degrees of specificity necessary for such complexity to exist. If this is not the case then the Darwinians need to explain how specificity/fine-tuning occurs through natural selection in the same manner as we are able to show the specificity of epigenetic (cell mediated) alterations to coding sequences.

Epigenetic Forms and Processes

Coding sequence modifications come in two forms: First, modifications that come through toxins or what are generally referred to as "mutations." These types of alterations can lead to disease states if not corrected. If the enzymes (DNMTs–DNA methyltransferases) necessary for correcting mistakes are damaged, then any future mutation(s) might not be corrected.

The other form of modification is internal or endocellular communication/selection and decision making. A major difference between mutations and endocellular selection is when the cell makes changes in response to decisions it likewise makes changes to other coding sequences of concern. Darwinian-type, random mutations don't do this, and can't do this, because they are not specific. How do we know? Because mutations of the Darwinian type are, again, random and haphazard; there is no intent of any kind behind a Darwinian mutation. Intent, however, does lie behind changes in coding sequences prompted by the cell itself; this is a will to life, a fight against death, entropy. Keep in mind the definitions under the term "mutation" in Chapter 1. In my opinion most of these mutation-types, that is, genetic drift, missense, nonsense, deletion, duplication, frame shifts and so on, are likely, in most instances, initiated by the cell. Transposition, or transposons, on the other hand, are likely viral in origin (but certainly cell mediated in some cases), a symbiotic issue I will get to shortly.

Endocellular Selection and Alterations in DNA

The life of cancer is complicated by the presence of trillions of microbes and their large number of signals. Microbes can benefit cancer cells but can also attack them. Like skin and gut lining cells, cancer cells must determine which microbes are friendly and converse with them. They must also evade attack from antagonistic species. . . .

Of trillions of microbes, ten types definitely are known to cause particular types of cancer. These microbes infect large numbers of people, *but cancer only appears in a small number of them*. Several bacteria are known to produce molecules that initiate cancer. Viruses initiate several cancer types by injecting RNA or DNA into human cells, sometimes placing them permanently in genes (Lieff 2020: 84). emphasis mine)

One of the recent revelations in cell biology was the ability of cancer cells to alter DNA. And, because cancer cells can alter DNA, it isn't a giant leap in realizing that healthy cells do this as well. The Darwinians believe this is all random and caused by extra-cellular activities. One of the many problems I have with this is the complexity of life and how this could be a strictly random adventure. This, actually, was one of the early criticisms of Darwin's ideas, but, in those days, without modern day technology, it was impossible to prove the point.

As pointed out by McFadden and Al-Khalili (2014:67-98), most of the communication between and within cells is carried out by enzymes. These include providing the means for chemicals to combine, bonds to occur between chemicals that would not ordinarily bond, tunneling, and so on. As McFadden and Al-Khalili comment (2014: 70):

> But are enzymes just biological catalysts, providing the same kind of chemistry that is used to make sulphuric acid and scores of other industrial chemicals? A few decades ago, most biologists would have agreed . . . that the chemistry of life is no different from the kinds of processes that take place inside a chemical plant, or even a child's chemistry set. But in the last couple of decades that view has radically changed as a number of key experiments have provided remarkable new insights into the way enzymes work. It seems that life's catalysts are able to reach down into a deeper level of reality than plain old classical chemistry and make use of some neat quantum trickery.

I have more to say on quantum biology in Chapter 6. At this point, keep in mind that it appears that decision making is not only part and parcel of the cells in an organism, the ultimate decision maker likely resides at the quantum level.

Biofilm and Exchange of Genetic Information

Biofilms exist almost everywhere in nature. They exist on almost every organ of the human body; all lifeforms are in one way or another part of biofilms.

> In nature, almost all microorganisms grow as part of communities attached to surfaces that are bathed by liquid, generally water. The organized surface-adherent communities are termed biofilms and are the way that bacteria and fungi grow on external and internal surfaces . . . In nature . . . biofilms are important in the pathogenesis of infectious diseases for several reasons. They protect the microbial community from host defenses, enable persistence of microbes in flowing systems such as blood and urine, protect microbes against desiccation, and, importantly, allow *efficient horizontal transfer of genes encoding virulent factors and resistance to antibiotics* (Cole 2020: 59). (emphasis mine)

The mantra in Darwinian evolution is bacteria, for example, randomly, accidently mutate and this is what leads to resistance to antibiotics. Resistance, however, may be initially epigenetic (cells thinking about the future, that is, preadaptations), and then the sharing of information resulting in a resistant strain; this has been scientifically verified.

An example of a biofilm is the slippery film that forms on and between your teeth and gums; brushing after meals and flossing usually breaks up most of this film but can never totally remove it. A multitude of bacteria, viruses, and so on, are imbedded in this film, and if not disturbed through brushing and flossing, it can lead to pockets between gums and teeth, bleeding gums, and dental carries. But it isn't all bad. Many of the bacteria in that film are useful and without them you can end up with severe oral hygiene problems.

These films are communities of bacteria, archaea, fungi, viruses, and so on, and they develop relationships with one another, exchanging information seeking immortality. The gut microbiome is of importance here. For microorganisms to survive they need a host, sometimes this is other bacteria, other times it is your intestinal walls and skin. Survival, then, depends on the survival of the host, and this means proper nutrition. Have you ever considered your food cravings? Where do these cravings come from? Somehow your brain and body (gut microbiome) communicate with the goal of fulfilling the need for a specific nutrient(s). The gut microbiome is part of the signaling system for food cravings, but the gut microbiome can have some potential negative effects, especially if you are malnourished, as most Westerners are.

Strandwitz comments (2018) in his Abstract:

The gut microbiota – the trillions of bacteria that reside within the gastrointestinal tract – has been found to not only be an essential component of immune and metabolic health, but also seems to influence development and diseases of the enteric and central nervous system, including motility disorders, behavioral disorders, neurodegenerative disease, cerebrovascular accidents, and neuroimmune-mediated disorders. By leveraging animal models, several different pathways of communication have been identified along the "gut-brain-axis" including those driven by the immune system, the vagus nerve, or by modulation of neuroactive compounds by the microbiota. Of the latter, bacteria have been shown to produce and/or consume a wide range of mammalian neurotransmitters, including dopamine, norepinephrine, serotonin, or gamma- aminobutyric acid (GABA). Accumulating evidence in animals suggests that manipulation of these neurotransmitters by bacteria may have an impact in host physiology, and preliminary human studies are showing that microbiota-based interventions can also alter neurotransmitter levels. Nonetheless, substantially more work is required to determine whether microbiota-mediated manipulation of human neurotransmission has any physiological implications, and if so, how it may be leveraged therapeutically.

It's possible that further research will reveal the part gut bacteria and viruses play in coding sequence starvation, and other responses by the gut-brain-axis.

We oversee a feral cat community (see Rush 2021) and over the years we experimented with different foods available in the market place. Our conclusion is, at least in terms of cats, they will, over time, go for the food that best serves their nutritional needs and avoid the other, unless the more nutritional food is unavailable. Now, cats can't read the labels on the packages and we can't tell them which is the most nutritious, so how do they know? Is it sight? Probably not, for cats don't see very well up close. They essentially see things with their faces, their whiskers. Is it smell or taste? Maybe, but how do they know? Possibly this information is sent by the gut, probably amplified by the microbiome and sent to the brain, most likely with a connection to the quantum world. Urbanized humans, however, in many cases do not consume food according to biological needs; we consume too much sugar, salt, and fat. Moreover, many of the available foods are packaged, and laced with salt, sugar, and fat, likely interfering with our innate ability to more specifically seek out the more nutritious foods; this leads to malnutrition over time and ill health.

Referring to the Dutch Hunger study, the body realized *nutrients*, not just calories, were missing and attempted to solve the problem by altering nutritional needs. This could have been through phase shifts and other endocellular coding sequence alterations preparing the next generation for survival within a different nutrient environment.

CHAPTER 6

Quantum Mechanics and Quantum Biology

"In physics, a quantum is the minimum amount of any physical entity involved in an interaction" (https://en.wikipedia.org/wiki/Quantum). At the quantum level we are dealing with codes, codes that borrow from one another, codes that have to be available at a "moments" notice, and codes with the appearance of being in a perpetual state of chaos. These codes seem to be written in vibrations, with waves (or strings) in continual movement at specific frequencies. The wave is a coherent state where all information is known throughout the wave, unlike a particle which might be considered a piece of the wave and information is limited to the particle. This is why, at the quantum level, all that is possible is in superposition, and with codes borrowing from other codes it would seem chaotic or disorganized, but it is not. We use the word chaotic for systems we don't understand. Weather systems are a good example. Although we are better able to predict weather conditions on a day-to-day basis – sometimes hour to hour, meteorologists only offer probabilities. Why? Because we don't know all the variables and thus can't factor them into the equation; we can't account for the butterfly flapping its wings in the Amazon. Some researchers assume the quantum level is random, but this can't be the case for emerging from the quantum level is structure and random doesn't create structure – codes create structure. The Darwinians believe order can be created out of disorder; my position is, when it comes to life, order comes out of order. We can invent math that says otherwise, but that math always begins with assumptions and this is investigator interference. The challenge for the Darwinians is to prove codes can be created randomly without the help of an intelligence. I can deliver tons of building materials and neatly stack them in some space. Left alone I guarantee you all the bits and pieces won't magically assemble into a house; in fact, most will disintegrate, and lose any order they had in the first place. I can pour all kinds of organic chemicals into a vessel and likewise they won't magically assemble into a functional protein, one used by lifeforms on this planet. We have conducted these experiments over and over and the results are the same, racemic amino acids, goo, and tar – no functional protein(s). Perhaps we need to simply wait several billion years, but, as the math informs, there isn't enough time in the whole age of the universe to randomly produce even *one*, single, solitary functional protein let alone all the other proteins to produce a single, self-replicating cell. Actually, a functioning protein by itself is useless unless it is joined with other proteins (enzymes, RNA, etc.) to produce a self-replicating unit, bacteria for example. How do the Darwinians explain this? There is no scientific explanation for the origins of life. For origin of species, there is scientific data, data that *contradicts* the Darwinian model.

Recently the US military released photos taken of UFOs being tracked by jet fighters. The technology apparently connected to these events is way beyond anything we are capable of, suggesting an intelligence, alien intelligence way beyond our wildest imaginings. If these objects are the product of lifeforms from other planets their intellectual abilities and technological development is also a sub-set of the energy that informs all. What this tells us is that we are far away from the ability to explain coding at the quantum level. We *think* we know about waves or strings at that level but we don't know how they exactly relate to one another.

Measurements have revealed numerous particles emerging from the wave form, which come under two general categories, three generations of fermions composed of leptons and quarks, and interacting forces or carriers called bosons. The first generation of quarks are up and down, we term the second-generation charm and strange, while we label the third generation top and bottom. For leptons, the first generation is composed of electron and election neutrino, the second, muon and muon neutrino, and the third generation, tau and tau neutrino. For the bosons we have gluon, photon, Z boson, W boson, and Higgs or H boson. The point: obviously there is a great deal of order existing within the wave form or, when measured, these arbitrarily named particles would not exist. Whether there are other particles remains to be seen. The question is, what is the wave form, that manifests as particles, doing during a dormant phase? With the complexity we see around us, I have difficulty imagining a static wave form. I think it reasonable to assume that eukaryote coding sequences in the wave form can rearrange sequences and create new possibilities. This also suggests that complex (irreducibly complex) genotypic or phenotypic changes only occur in the wave form. Thus, for example, the differences in a quadrupedal vs bipedal knee joint do not occur after the wave form has collapsed. Individual alterations to coding sequences may occur during the collapsed phase (e.g., alteration of a nucleotide from C to T, or A to G) but large changes, because of their complexity, occur in the wave form during dormant phases. This may explain the existence of new life forms after a catastrophic event. Again, this is only speculation (Rush 2020: 186-187).

Keep in mind that physicists may not have identified all the particles. The thinking is, if they do find a new particle it likely has a partner. My intuition tells me that the Higgs boson has a partner that has not been identified. If this turns out to be correct I want first dibs on calling it the *Sean boson*, a good Irish name; I'm sure Darwin would approve. But the Higgs may be a single "particle," without a mate. I envisage the quantum world like a story, with many players and possible endings. And all stories need a "storyteller," or "someone" who pulls the characters together and decides the ending. In quantum mechanics the Higgs boson might be the master particle (or wave) that orchestrates the tangible world. To do such a thing represents a complexity far beyond our understanding.

The fact that we can measure particles that emerge from the waveform indicates that these particles "create" the tangible world we experience. The coding at the quantum level, then, is in perpetual, dynamic equilibrium, and to be understood requires a math beyond our current capabilities. Classical physics, math, and chemistry help us to understand the tangible world, but the major "tools" for explaining the quantum world haven't been invented as yet, and, unless we develop a different type of brain power, one that will take us to another level of intelligence, we are stuck in the classical world of physics and math. I think that once we do understand the quantum level we will have become it.

The one thing that does seem to bring the quantum and classical worlds together is *consciousness* (see my earlier discussion on consciousness and awareness). We are getting into metaphysics here, and that's okay, as long as we don't turn it into fact.

Lanza (2020: 19-22) states, in terms of the Third principle of biocentrism:

> The behavior of subatomic particles – indeed all particles and objects – is inextricably linked to the presence of an observer. Absent a conscious observer, they best exist in an undetermined state of probability waves.

So, what is it about consciousness that allows this connection between the classical and quantum worlds and forces the classical world into existence? The philosophical issue is this: without an observer all is in *superposition* or all possible configurations at once. It doesn't mean the world we experience doesn't exist, but without an observer, how would we know? How can you possibly prove this without measurement? But with measurement the wave form collapses and can't be measured. The big problem is we don't really understand where our consciousness comes from. We say the brain, but what part of the brain? Is consciousness merely a part of brain/chemical functioning, or is consciousness something that comes from *outside in* rather than strictly inside out? Hoffman (2019: 150):

> For a theory that proposes that brain activity causes conscious experiences, we want mathematical laws or principles that state precisely which brain activities cause the conscious experience of tasting basil, precisely why this activity does not cause the experience of, say, hearing a siren, and precisely why this activity must change to transform the experience from tasting basil to, say, tasting rosemary. These laws or principles must apply across species, or else explain precisely why different species require different laws. No such laws, indeed no plausible ideas, have ever been proposed.

Actually, McFadden and Al-Khalili (2014) do present some interesting possibilities, specifically with taste and smell, dealing with enzymes and the quantum domain. In any case, the math and understanding would have to reside within the quantum realm, it is within us, just as calculus, geometry, and so on, are within us, were realized by the mind, communicated to others, and eventually written down. It is right in front of us but it will require a different type of thinking to codify it and pass it on to others. Perhaps we are too thoroughly grounded in our math models to appreciate that which stares us in the face.

Dreaming and the Quantum Level

The quantum level is likely accessed during dream states (see Rush 2020: 77, 137), and, instead of attempting to understand dreams as reference to neurosis, personality, or some other psychiatric or psychological disorder, perhaps we should attempt to understand their possible connection to the quantum level with fresh eyes. Conceivably quantum math is imbedded in dream, which would also include deep meditation and hypnosis. I say this because all things can be referenced at once in a dream. Time is not an issue and you can be in different places at the same "time." Time while dreaming is almost always compressed, that is, what seems to go on forever is often just a few minutes or even seconds. Problems are even solved when dreaming. Although dreaming can have a liner "feel" to it, the images can be incongruent representing a multitude of "things" at once. When we recall dreams in the conscious/awareness state, they usually don't make much sense, although they seem perfectly logical during the dream state. Dreaming, along with deep meditation and hypnosis, may be as close as we can get to "measuring" the quantum level without creating decoherence or collapse (waves "become" particles) of the wave form.

In dreams we see things – objects, people, pets, just as we would see them when awake. What is presented is matched to our senses. But this is not the way things really are at the quantum level. Images in your dreams are wave forms expressed so you can interpret them; dreams do not appear to be particles – I'm not sure you can capture a particle of a dream. With that said, perhaps this is why we dream, to acquaint us with the quantum level and maybe in time we can make sense out of the images in terms of mathematical formulas. Meditation, hypnosis, and certain drugs might also be useful tools for accessing that level of awareness.

Quantum Biology

Quantum biology is the application of quantum mechanics to the mechanisms of origin and maintenance of life. Originally, research didn't think the quantum level could be attributed to lifeforms. As Mohsen et al. (2015: xvii) state:

> Biological systems tend to be warm, wet and noisy (the latter because they are exposed to environmental fluctuations), conditions which are normally expected to result in rapid decoherence and thus suppression of quantum features. Therefore, quantum phenomena may at first sight seem to be unlikely to play a significant role in biology.

Scientists now know this is not true. Continuing the definition, Fleming and Scholes (2015: 3) comment:

If we set aside the fact that quantum mechanics is required to explain the properties of molecules and their reactions – obviously important in biochemical processes ranging from the action of enzymes to genetic expression of phenotypes and the very construction of a living organism – then *quantum biology* identifies biological phenomena that make explicit use of quantum mechanics to attain functionality or to carry out a process.

To date much of the research in quantum biology has centered on photosynthesis light-harvesting, vision, olfaction/taste, and magneto-reception but is likewise applicable to "cell photoprotection using melanin, bioluminescence and sophisticated sunscreens used by coral" (Fleming and Scholes 2015: 6; see also Kim, et al. 2021 for updated information).

. . . Erwin Schrodinger, in his famous book *What is Life?* noted that quantum mechanics accounts for the stability of living things and their cellular processes because of our understanding, via quantum mechanics, of the stability and structure of molecules. The fact that quantum effects create, sometimes large, energy gaps between different states of a chemical system is also important. Such energy gaps, between electronic energy levels, enable living organisms to capture and store the energy carried from the sun by photons, and to visualize the world around them via optically induced chemical reactions (Fleming and Scholes 2015: 3).

The Concept of Open Systems

In order for functional endocellular selection to occur there has to be an interface with the external world. Shabani, et al. (22015: 14) comment:

. . . Natural systems are open to the exchange of particles, energy or information with their surrounding environments that often have complex structures. Therefore, the theory of open quantum systems plays a key role in dynamical modeling of quantum-biological systems. Research in quantum biology and open quantum system theory have found a bilateral relationship.

By "bilateral relationship" the authors indicate a "give and take" of information between the cell and the environment. This is not a one-way street as environed by the Darwinians. In order for a two-way street to be meaningful, information input has to be interpreted and followed by decisions, likely offered at the quantum level, as to how to proceed. Some researchers say this is all automatic, simply "instinctive" chemical reactions, stimulus and automatic response. The answer to that is, there are many possibilities, not just one reaction, response, or outcome, and this requires decisions and *various* reactions for the diverse outcomes. An automatic decision-tree type analysis of the information won't work – it's too slow.

How does this inside-outside communication work? What goes on at the cellular (inside) level after information is received? Part of the answer involves enzymes which have a large part to play in allowing information diffusion into and out of the quantum world.

The quantum level is a sea of rules, or mathematical constructs, a math that hasn't bubbled up from the brain to the mind to explain this realm. Or, perhaps it has (maybe it has in dreams), but no one is enlightened enough to "see" it. We need a few more Plancks, Einsteins, or Schrodingers; we need a creativity that is open and not fettered or grounded in Darwinism and the current math, physics, and chemistry models. This is not any easy request.

As mentioned, time and space, at least from my interpretation, are irrelevant in the quantum world. The coding at this level is such that all life forms that can be imagined, as long as they follow rules, are possible. Yockey (2005:184) states:

> . . . The genetic information system operates without regard or the specificity of the message because it must be capable of handling all genetic messages of all organisms, extinct and living,

as well as those not yet evolved. That is possible only because the message in the genome is segregated, linear, and digital. This shows without a doubt that evolution and genetics cannot be understood except by information theory.

If the quantum level runs on random, then its ability to carry, store, or utilize information would be very low. This can't possibly be the case when you consider the complexity of life that surrounds us.

CHAPTER 7

The God Issue

I don't have a personalized god. I do not subscribe to Judaism, Christianity, Islam, Buddhism, and so on; I've spent many years studying these systems, I think they are fascinating and culturally informative, but I'm not a member. I advocate, know thyself, seek wisdom, and be a decent person; any deities demanding worship along with this would qualify as demons. Think about it. If there is a god, or energy that informs all, with super intelligence and capabilities, this entity would have to be *enormously* insecure to demand worship.

Be that as it may, I think people should be able to believe what they want; belittling a person's beliefs is culturally insensitive. How they *practice* their religion, for example, going around converting people, or marginalizing or murdering those that refuse to join, turns these traditions into fascist political systems and not spiritual adventures. Believing in a personalized god is really the same as being an atheist, as both rely on faith, and neither one can prove their case. You cannot prove that something doesn't exit, like an energy that informs all, so there is always a "perhaps."

With that said, one has to wonder why the thought of an intelligence beyond that of the human animal strikes so much fear in the hearts of Darwinians? Certainly, any space aliens coming to this planet are much smarter than us. In fact, we should be gravely concerned about such visitors as they can probably destroy civilization as we know it. Large systems, like a nation-state, are inherently unstable.

The concept of god, or energy that informs all, doesn't stop science. Only in some of the extreme religious sects does dogma stop investigations of Nature. Speaking of extreme groups, those in academia who prevent the discussion of other possibilities besides Darwinism, have acted much the same as the Catholic Church once it assumed power. I can understand Darwin and others needing to undermine the creation story because the power of the Church prevented the public from having a story other than that offered by the Judeo-Christian tradition, but *we are past that*. Controlling information dissemination becomes a political issue and this is one of the problems connected to the Darwinians – they are politicians, not scientists. Scientists inform. They present the data for people to accept or reject. Politicians manipulate information; they present data to crush their opponents and insure re-election. More about our small group nature, the need to control information, and Darwinism in Chapter 8.

When we speak of religion we are also assuming worship and/ or ritual expression of the beliefs. I believe that an energy informs this universe but, in my opinion, it is not a reference for worship and ritual. According to Meyer (2021: 219-222) there are four basic theories as to the origin of the universe and life, materialism or naturalism, pantheism, theism, and deism.

> Philosophers recognize several main worldviews with different answers to this ultimate, or "prime reality," question. "Naturalism" (or materialism) views matter and energy and the laws of nature as the prime realities. "Pantheism" asserts an impersonal deity present in matter and energy as the prime reality. "Theism" affirms a personal, intelligent, transcendent God who also acts within the creation. And "deism" affirms a personal, transcendent, intelligent God who does *not* act within the created order after its initial origin . . .

Using Bayesian logic Meyer concludes that the "God Hypothesis" (pantheism, theism, and deism) is a better explanation for origins of the universe and life within it (Meyer 2021: 239-278). The major support for his conclusion is the existence of a finite universe, as determined by cosmologists, a universe that began at a certain point in time and space. If this is the case, and it appears to be so, where did this come from? In materialistic science, causes are not irrelevant, so what "caused" the universe? Outside of saying, "God did it," any details are metaphysical – which seems to be appropriate in science today, but only if you are recognized as a person in the know, an authority figure of some sort, like Dawkins (2017), Krauss (2013), Carroll (2019), or Kaku (2021). So, in my opinion, if these noted scholars can spout metaphysics, then so can the "God did it" crowd. The fact is, we just don't know. But not knowing the origins of the universe should not stop us from determining as much as we can, with our limited intelligence, about how it all works. If there is an intelligence behind the origin of the universe, we, and all other lifeforms, are a subset of this intelligence. And, that's okay – it's nice to belong.

The underlying issue here, however, is political for any suggestion of an intelligence beyond that of the human animal or other lifeforms in the universe, threatens the atheist position and the belief that morality is merely a social construct; this relieves guilt. Such a position allows the elite to treat people as they see fit. Morality, however, is not "merely" a social construct – *it is a social necessity*. I would have difficulty accepting that anyone reading this believes that lying, cheating, stealing, physically and mentally abusing individuals or groups are irrelevant issues in terms of group functioning. A culture's philosophy of life either binds members and groups together or pulls them apart.

Order and Illusion

The faith driven atheists would have us believe the order we perceive in systems, in Nature in general, came out of disorder. The thinking is, if all came from disorder then there is no purpose; it just happened. Purpose, or why the universe and life exist, produces interesting philosophy. As humans, many of us are trying to make sense of our experiences and in most cases the best we can do is tell stories.

And the story for the Darwinians is wrapped around the need for randomness to create the universe and all the lifeforms within, but without a scientific explanation of where the universe came from in the first place. If the universe emerged out of disorder, where did all this "disorder" come from and what caused the disorder to spontaneously evolve into order? The answer to this is, given enough time disorder turns into order. All the rules of the universe, expressed by humans in an exquisite, symbolic form called mathematics, came from disorder randomly creating order. All the DNA and RNA molecules along with all the enzymes and architecture came from disorder randomly creating order. The Darwinians simply accept that randomness caused the universe, and all the life within, on faith. To circumvent this, some academics start with a different premise, that is, the universe emerged from nothing; there was no disorder, something (the universe) came from nothing.

To date there is no scientific proof of origins of the universe. Removing the interference of a researcher, how can you prove that random mutations can create codes? That is *the* challenge and I don't see any of the Darwinians steeping up with proof. I personally think the concept of random mutations coupled with natural selection and time producing life and new species is a magnificent and enduring illusion created by the Darwinians.

Emotions and Information Storage

If the environment gave you emotions, you would not be able to override the associated behaviors, behaviors could never be spontaneous, and decision making would never occur. Most languages contain one of the most powerful defense mechanisms ever invented. It is called emotional *irresponsibility*; with emotional irresponsibility you can blame everything that happens, not on your behavior, but on everyone else. We reference emotions as given to us by the other, which could be a person, object, or acts of Nature. "Stop it! You're making me angry!" "That book is very interesting!" "That's a beautiful sunset!" Nothing can make you angry, a book can't be interesting, and a sunset can't be beautiful – beauty is in the mind of the beholder, to borrow an old expression. This feeds into the idea of random mutations and natural selection; like emotions, our language clearly states that emotions are given to you, like a pen or piece of paper. And just like emotions we have *no* control over random mutations or natural selection; they control the game of life. We are helpless.

When we step away from this linguistic illusion we recognize the individual is "given" information, or an experience, which is interpreted by the individual using history, some of which is inherited (innate releasing mechanisms, perhaps), along with the original emotion used to store the information/experience.

Nature is only the messenger; Nature does not instruct how to change or evolve. This change potential, in response to the message of Nature, has to derive from within the cell, from within the organism. If, on the other hand, Nature is instructing the cell/organism, then this suggests an intelligence, an energy source compelling Nature to create the "fittest." If, on the other side, Nature is only a messenger without a boss, then endocellular selection has to be in play. I don't think you can have this both ways. Consciousness and consequent awareness of organisms are the "eyes and ears" of evolution; awareness informs the cell and, through a complicated information processing system involving the quantum level, the cell decides. From this we also learn cells *can't* predict the future, only anticipate, in a similar fashion, humans can't predict the future, but we can anticipate. Part of this may be what we call "intuition" or "gut" feeling in some cases. Perhaps that is the elders speaking to us from the quantum world – just a thought.

One purpose of language is to reinforce ideas, offer collaboration of our experiences, solve problems, and test and verify beliefs. With respect to the study of the origin of life, the origin of species, and the origins of our kind we need to be open to all possibilities and not get trapped into believing a story just because it has been told over and over again. It comes down to the desire to be a scientist or a politician.

CHAPTER 8

Why Do We Still Preach Darwinism?

The History

So, how did we get to this place where an elite (Charles Darwin) creates a story, a good story, that is not allowed to be challenged by science? Richard Dawkins, like Darwin, presents anecdote after anecdote "proving" random mutations and natural selection brought all life forms into existence, but there is no science to back it up, only stories or descriptions of end products without a clear statement (math, physics, chemistry) about how lifeforms change and new species emerge. In order to answer the question of "why" we still preach Darwin, we have to examine a number of subjects. One is myth, and how it directs our thinking. Others include the development of culture, our small group nature, and how small groups control larger groups. The major concern for control in large groups, just as the cells in your body, is the *control of information*. Let me set the scene and then I'll tell my story.

Mathematics, Randomness, and the Origins of life

In the 1960s (see Moorhead and Kaplan 1967) mathematical calculations revealed that it would be impossible for even one, small functional protein to be randomly created during the age of the universe. There are some problems with the math, but in 1972, using calculations based on *equilibrium thermodynamics*, Prigogine at al. (1972: 31) concluded:

The probability that at ordinary temperatures a macroscopic number of molecules is assembled to give rise to the highly ordered structures and to the coordinated functions characterizing living organisms is vanishingly small. The idea of spontaneous genesis of life in its present form is therefore highly improbable even on the scale of the billions of years during which prebiotic evolution occurred.

Thaxton et al. (1986: 164) comment further regarding the processes necessary to create a functioning protein, that is, the energy to create order *and* energy to turn order into functioning complexity – these are two separate, but interrelated issues:

> We must not forget that the total work to create a living system goes far beyond work to create DNA and protein . . . As we have stated before, a minimum of 20-40 proteins as well as DNA and RNA are required to make even a simple replicating system. The lack of known energy-coupling means to do the configurational entropy work required to make DNA and protein is many times more crucial in making a living system. As a result, appeals to chance for this most difficult problem still appear in the literature in spite of the fact that calculations give staggeringly low probability, even the scale of 5 billion years. Either the work – especially the organizational work – was coupled to the flow of energy in some way not yet understood, or else it truly was a miracle.

So, we have the Darwinian storyline where random mutations create codes and complex life forms, and the laws of thermodynamics are wrong, **OR** random mutations creating complex life is wrong, and thermodynamics is right. They both can't be correct (see Thaxton 1986: 127-143).

The point is scientists have known for many decades that random, spontaneous origins of life are improbable at best. As Thaxton et al. comment (1986: 5), "It cannot be denied that the 'pure chance' view of the origin of life is a position of extreme faith." The Darwinian position has been maintained, not out of stupidity or ignorance, but out of fear of upsetting the political direction the Darwinian position pushed Western culture (see Rush 2020). Thus, we reach a point where the question needs to be asked, can we trust scientists to tell the truth, to be open minded, and consider all possibilities regarding the origin of life and new species? The answer at the junction in history is, no. A great deal of data is withheld from textbooks offering alternate explanations. This is one method of controlling information (school text books) in order to steer belief patterns in a particular direction. This, then sets the stage for exploring myth, and how it directs our thinking, and exploring origins of culture and our small group nature.

Mythmaking and the Origin of Species

Storytelling and mythmaking have a long season, hero myths in particular (see Campbell 1973). There are several types of heroes, including the one who slays (i.e. Mithras, Darwin, etc.), the one who is slain (i.e. Jesus, Bruce Willis [*Armageddon*], etc.), and the community as hero (i.e. Jewish tradition, although we do have heroes within the general storyline, i.e. Samson, etc.). Heroes are important because they represent the energy of society and many times the direction society "should" take to solve problems.

One of my favorite hero myths is, *Mickey and the Beanstalk*, that wonderful cartoon by Walt Disney. The hero in this case is a triplet hero with Mickey representing mind (intelligence, cunning, etc.), Goofy (the body), and Donald Duck, who represents emotion, raw emotion, that has to be tempered by the body and mind.

Anyway, as Disney's rendition of the story goes, our heroes, and the townsfolk, have a problem – their magic harp was stolen, and without her magical song, the vitality of the community will dry up, dissipate (entropy). Facing starvation, and after an emotional outburst by Donald, Mickey takes the family cow to market. But mysteriously, on the way to market, he meets a traveling salesman, a magical helper, and trades the cow for some magic beans. When Goofy and Donald hear what Mickey has done, in a rage, Donald knocks the beans from Mickey's hand, they bounce along the floor – ping, ping, ping, ping, and fall down an interesting looking knot hole – plunk!

You see, Mickey, Goofy, and Donald represent the community, the towns folk, and they can't solve the problem locally. A journey of some type is necessary in order to find, or, in this case retrieve what the community has lost or needs in order to move forward. Thus, we need a magic helper, the salesman but more importantly the magic beans, to transport our heroes to that other place, a place that will provide what they need to bring order to their community. Back to the story.

As the full moon shines on the knot hole, the beans sprout and grow into an immense, intertangled beanstalk. During the rapid growth phase our heroes are subject to their *night journey*, moving up, up, and up with the beanstalk, a journey into the night sky filled with all kinds of dangers! Passing through all the dangers unscathed, our heroes immerge in the morning in front of a huge castle in the sky surrounded by a moat, which they begin to cross in a bean pod, but are swamped as a gigantic fish eats a enormous mosquito! But they make it to shore, "the hard way!"

In the castle lived a giant, actually a shape-shifting ogre, who had stolen the magic harp for his own personal pleasure; ogres apparently like music. Overcoming numerous obstacles, the three heroes obtain the harp, make their way down the beanstalk, slay the giant who disrupted social functioning, return the harp and vitality and life to the community, and everyone lives happily ever after in Happy Valley.

The Darwin Myth
The Darwinian myth follows the same sequence as in most hero myths. Our young privileged hero, Darwin, has no direction in life. He has tried to find his way in medicine and so on, but he is lost. He likes

to play with things in nature, bugs and such, but he has no real focus. He is searching for the meaning (origins) of life and what he wants and needs can't be found locally; locally there is only talk.

So, with "magical" help (a former professor, John Steven Henslow), our hero gets on a boat (H.M.S. Beagle – his long journey to another place), has to face many obstacles for many long months (his "night journey"), and ultimately reaches his island destination. He has insects to fight, malnutrition, and unfriendly natives, and finally, after many months, he has the proof he'd been looking for.

But his journey is not over yet, for many miles separate him from his homeland and those who would receive his proof of origin of species. A long sea voyage, poor food, unfriendly shipmates, and after five years, he returns home and presents his findings to the world. The "dragon" called religion has been slain with the sword of random mutations and natural selection. Soon our hero's name would be a household word, honored by some, reviled by others, but our hero's message will echo in the halls of academia as truth, that is, random mutations plus natural selection plus time equals new species. Amen.

The story of Darwin has been told so often, repeated in textbook after textbook to the point where it is like a prayer, a ritual, and any opposition is swiftly dealt with. The thinking of the Darwinians is simple – if you disagree with Darwin you must be a religious or Intelligent Design fanatic! Intelligent Design, as mentioned, has nothing to do with religion, as religion involves worship and ritual, none of which are part of Intelligent Design. Intelligent Design, or rather the research involved, was hijacked by organized religion in order to "prove" the existence of their personalized gods, but ID, originally, had nothing to do with gods, goddess, angels, or demons. It came about through scientific observations. Information has been "spun" and distorted by the Darwinians in order to demonize the competition; a typical political move. Gossip and rumor are used as well to marginalize those not "towing the line" (the school unions are expert at this), a common religious and/or political ploy. This definitely happens in the halls of academia.

Our Small Group Nature, Power, and Persistence of a Myth

Keep in mind that culture is like a generic, a platform from which to build variations. What are the very basic elements, the platform necessary for the development of human culture? What does that have to do with myth, and how does our small group nature fit into this? I outlined this many years ago (see Rush 1996 and 1999) as a response to Freud's model (Freud 1990), a "just so" story, a ridiculous creation story (the creation of culture) that is still referenced in the psychiatric community, and held onto as well by many psychologists.

To begin, Freud was an atheist and his storyline was designed to show that morality is a social *invention* stemming *from* religion, also an invention. Morality is a *social necessity* if people are to cooperate in their small groups – without guidelines for behavior, group survival is limited. Any psychiatrist, even in Freud's day, should know this. Once again, the Freudian model is faith-based, with no scientific validity, that passes as truth because it came from the mind of an elite. Malinowski (1927, 1929), a British social anthropologist, early on, poked all kinds of holes in Freud's storyline, and even to this day some anthropologists still believe the Freudian narrative. This shows how powerful myth can be especially if it is backed by some perceived authority figure(s) and told over, and over, and over again – repetition is important for anchoring in specific messages.

Freud's Myth

Briefly, Freud's story is one where a grand old man has access to all the women and the young men are kept outside the group. At some point they get very frustrated, because, most likely, they "aren't getting any." So, they kill the father, eat him, and then have sex with all the women.

At some point of satiation these young men sit on a hot rock and experience guilt – "Oh, what have we done?" They realize they have killed their father (and ate him), and had sex with their sisters and mothers. They are devastated, so shocked by their actions they invent totemism, where their most favorite food item becomes a symbol for the father, and is off limits – this equals "religion" and food taboos. Next, they invent exogamy where the only women they can have are from other groups. Here he confused exogamy, marrying outside the group, with sex, which are two entirely different adventures. So, in one fell swoop he invents consciousness (guilt), "religion" (totemism), and sexual restriction rules. Did this just happen once and diffuse throughout the world or is there independent invention involved? There is absolutely no proof anywhere that such events actually occurred, so we have a good bedtime story. But, it became a therapeutic issue, or basis for dealing with the Oedipus complex, of the son's antagonisms toward the father. In his private practice, Freud frequently encountered men who hated their fathers, and loved their mothers, because of the harsh discipline many fathers meted out to their sons, which was common in a strictly male dominated society of his time. He considered discipline normal and missed the part about how the child might react to being beaten and rejected and, instead, invented an elaborate story assuming "father hate" was deeply imbedded in the male human psyche (he didn't have much to say about women). Of course, if this wasn't resolved by the time of puberty it would mean five hours a week on the psychiatrist's couch, at whatever the going rate was back then.

Moreover, Freud relied on myth when outlining his position, and, with respect to the Oedipus myth (and the "Oedipus complex"), had he been aware of and read the original Greek Oedipus stories, he never would have come to the same conclusions.

I never accepted Freud's storyline and decided to take a close look at the basic and necessary elements for constructing what we would call human culture. By the mid-1980s, I constructed another model which also helped to explain why certain stories tend to persist in "science" when contrary data, from lots of scientific experiments, is available. This has a lot to do with our small group nature and the rituals and stories we tell for reinforcing our identity and loyalty to the group. Let me preface this with I'm not sure how what I'm going to present came about but I suspect it happened early on, certainly before *Homo erectus*-types (it may have been an Australopithecine, although I am doubtful) left Africa around 3 MYA. I think these elements came about out of necessity; if they were going to survive they all had to be on the same page, so to speak, play by the same rules. Dominance hierarchies are a part of primate social organization so, I suppose, it was a matter of refining that which already existed.

Growing Culture

There are nine basic ingredients necessary for cultural development in my model which I've broken up into three triads. However, my model presupposes the use of some type of language, perhaps not like language as we know it, but good enough to talk about events and store information symbolically (words, phrases, gestures), before culture could emerge with all the elements listed below.

The First Triad

In the First Triad we encounter consciousness, duality, and analogous thinking. Duality and analogous thinking are part of our consciousness/awareness but I've separated them to make a point.

Consciousness – Many have attempted to define consciousness; I went into this in some detail (see Rush 1996) with the conclusion that no one knows what it is or where it comes from. It was once thought to occur in or between the synapses in the brain, but it is possible that it occurs within the neurons themselves, or perhaps it comes from outside in. As mentioned, consciousness is like a light bulb, it is either on or off. My concern is with *awareness*, as awareness can lead to understanding, interpretation, and possible action. I coupled this with the basic research model used in cultural anthropology, and that is participant/observer. In other words, we have a consciousness that allows awareness, which in turn allows us to be *part of Nature* (we participate) and to recognize we are also *apart from Nature* (observers – we observe ourselves in relation to our surroundings). How our consciousness happens, I don't have a clue. But, without consciousness and resulting awareness nothing exists – the material world only emerges, apparently, with a conscious observer. This concept has been around since the early 1920s (the Copenhagen Interpretation, crafted between 1925 to 1927 by Niels Bohr and Werner Heisenberg in Copenhagen, Denmark, although parts of this concept are certainly metaphysical). According to Lanza (2020), it is consciousness that knits together the classical world of physics and quantum mechanics.

Duality – Without the ability to step back and make note of one's experiences, culture as we know it cannot exist. Along with this we appear to live in a dualistic world, with up and down, in and out, male and female, and so on. While in the womb the fetus is aware of stressors, some of which originate outside the womb. Duality probably begins in the womb as the fetus senses itself in relation to stressors and coding sequences (genes) as the male or female develops (male and female are important because they likely react differently to different stressors, even in the womb). I can predict this because of epigenetics and the ability of the fetus to recognize when alterations are to be made and modify coding sequences as it develops. The fetus, however, may not be aware of his or her mother.

Analogous Thinking – Also connected to awareness is analogous thinking or when one thing can stand for another. Here we are into symbolism, where a log can be a chair, or a cave a house. A more specific symbolic rendering, although controversial, is the analogous relationship between stone tools and the teeth of predators, especially the Acheulean hand axe (see Wynn 1989 and Rush 1996), dated to around 1.8 MYA, which is similar in shape to both canines and carnassial molars. If this is true then we have our first evidence of symbolic rendering and a mythological breeding ground for "stealing the power" of the predators who not only ate our ancestors but also provided them food in the form of animal carcasses to scavenge (see Rush 2021). However, if there was one symbolic/analogous rendering there were likely to be others not detected during excavations and analysis. Spoken words don't leave particles in the dust.

In any case, it is through analogous thinking and symbolism, most likely referenced in spoken language, that would allow our ancestors to leave Africa. Without language ability to *apply* analogous thinking our ancestors were unlikely to appreciate new plants, their edibility and medical qualities, and unable to store that information, through language, for transport to the next generation. This is one reason chimps can't leave Africa on their own; they don't possess the degree of analogous thinking, or linguistic abilities/strategies, found in our Homo ancestors to appreciate new foods (chimps are stuck in Africa because they need fruit), and without language the next generation would have to reinvent the wheel, so to speak. Experience has to be stored, retrieved, and transmitted intergenerationally in order to aid in survival, otherwise, like smoke, it drifts away in the breeze.

Second Triad

Food Sharing – The second triad contains food sharing, home base, and sexual restrictions. Food sharing is a must, and although other animals share food it is not on a continual basis. Knowing you are going to have a meal is part of the group bond, an acknowledgement of acceptance. The origins of this behavior are likely prompted by analogous thinking, that is mother sharing food with child.

The pair bond, if there really is such a thing, is connected to sex and the emotions that surround that behavior. Male/female bonds have a short life expectancy; the reasons for this will become evident as I proceed.

The mother/child bond, as mentioned, is perhaps the starting off point for food sharing in general. The human animal, when compared to pigs or cats, has few offspring, usually a single birth, but sometimes twins. And a survival strategy was chosen, in conjunction with few births, to invest a great deal of time and energy in our children. This starts off with breast feeding, and, about 12 to 18 months later, the child becomes mobile and learns how to forage, what to eat and what to avoid, and to share with others. This behavior, first the breast feeding, a form of sharing, then foraging, with mother sharing food with infant, establishes an implied rule (discussed more fully in the Third Triad), that is, "share food," and this becomes expected and ritualized. Our ancestors lived in small groups, and the members either cooperate or die. The idea of a cave man dragging his mate around by the hair is ridiculous. Brutality toward group members ends in morale problems, stress, and possible violence. For the guy dragging the girl around by the hair, he, at some point, is going to have to sleep and he might not wake up.

What I find interesting is the time period of 12 to 18 months when the infant is a little less dependent on his or her mother, and the weakening of the "pair bond," the bond between mother and father. Male infatuation for the other begins to wane within 12 to 18 months. Prior to this time the mother is vulnerable to predation or not acquiring enough energy to support herself or her child, and the next generation, that bridge to immortality, might be eliminated. Having the support of a male (or mother, sisters, or other members of the group) increases survival potential. Moreover, males can spread their genetic information around; women can't do this – pregnancy is dangerous. She can only get pregnant once every 9-12 months; men can impregnate women any hour of the day (or night). I can only speculate on the survival value of such behavior, that is, the waning of the "pair bond," and interest in other sexual mates. It certainly assures that male coding sequences will go marching on. As I suggested in Chapter 4, the alteration of hormones (pheromones) may have something to do with maintaining the bond once the female is pregnant, but testosterone levels begin to normalize at least by 12 to 18 months later. So, the male-female pair bond may have to do with alterations in pheromones, and the alterations also may explain why the male's "roving eye" returns to him after the infant is less dependent on the male/female bond for survival.

For the female, her coding sequences will go marching on in any case. It seems to work like this, except in cases of rape, women always know when they will have sex; the male can never be sure – he has to be invited in. Women, in this respect, teach men patience.

Keeping this in mind it isn't too big of a stretch to say that, at least for the human female, she is the true operator is Darwin's sexual selection. Strict sexual restriction rules and rape, along with arranged marriages aside, in the West, it is the woman who choses with whom she will have sex. And one would think that, according to the rules of natural selection, women will choose the most "fit" men. How do we define "fit?" Are we talking tall, dark, and handsome? Are we talking the ability to provide? Are we talking the nicest car, political connections, or length of the chosen one's penis? As poets have conceded for a few thousand years, the heart knows what it wants, and this may have nothing to do fitness, a term so general as to be useless. For humans, sexual selection, in my opinion, is in the hands of women, and choices for "love" are not necessarily rational or related to fitness, whatever that turns out to be.

Home Base – Nighttime was dangerous for our ancestors and, as with other primates, home bases are established for sleeping, eating, planning, protection, and so on. This also opens the door for the development of *group rituals* that further enhance bonding of group members. In the Western world there are rituals surrounding leaving home base (home, office) and returning to home base, the boardroom, or any location that is frequently revisited. Here we are into rhythmic activities, with individual and cooperative activities ritualized, where everyone joins in. Ritual is a seriously important issue when it comes to maintaining the bonds between members of our small groups; bonds need to be reinforced.

Keep in mind our ancient ancestors traveled in small groups, probably not more than 50 individuals at any one time, usually much less. Any territory will produce only so many calories, and when group membership reaches a certain point, consumable calories are limited, stress increases, and the group splits. This may be the origin of clans, or song lines (Australia), an identity for interaction in the future. This also spreads groups out and the development of new phenotypes in time. However, at certain times of the year (or longer cycles) food is plentiful in certain areas and groups may come back together. Recontact and hybridization, after many generations in particular, is a key to survival and acquiring novel coding sequences that could add in survival over time and the development of new species.

Sexual Restrictions – All cultures have sexual and marriage restrictions of one type or another and the reason centers around the powerful emotions connected to procreation. The goal of sexual restrictions is related to keeping stress low in the group. Most cultures in their rules and regulations promote marriage; everyone will have a mate. Let's look at this in more detail.

First, there is a "will to life," and that "will" doesn't leave much to chance. The human animal, like every other mammal on this planet, sends out signals, invitations for sexual interludes. For the human male there is facial hair, pheromones, low voice tone, and muscle. And, of course, it doesn't hurt to have "proper" body shape and clear skin. There are other physical considerations but It also helps, at least in the West, to have a fat wallet and/or political connections. It doesn't take much for men to get all excited – all the other has to do, in most cases, is just show up. But aside from the fact that "men are easy," women have their own signals to attract males. A smile is perhaps enough, unless she wishes to "capture" a particular male, then there are breasts, buttock, thin ankles, pheromones, and voice tone. I have even heard stories about women having a "love drug" in their biofilms, on the skin, lips, and other mucus membranes. Supposedly this "love drug" serves to break the bond between the former mate. In any event, perhaps it is just the pheromones given off in her scent.

One of the signaling problems men face, at least in North America, is that it is politically incorrect to ogle women (perhaps it is considered visual assault?), to be transfixed by the signals endocellular selection has provided; I guess it is a sign of disrespect. The male is to make eye-to-eye contact only; no "looking at the girls!" We aren't supposed to look at the other as a sex object; tell that to Mother Nature! These signals, both male and female, are part of the will to life and immortality, *not immorality*. Sociologists, at least in the past, considered potential mate watching a learned behavior but most is simply that deep-down need to become immortal, and in order to do that, men need women, and women need men, and they make choices based on signal preferences. The point. It doesn't take much for the human male to get excited about a woman, any woman, and he is not a good candidate for monogamy. We hear of the wandering eye and many books have been written on how to "keep your man," with the advice usually surrounding sex. Now, I'm not trying to excuse men's behavior; I'm trying to explain it. Women, on the other side, do most of the work; pregnancy can kill you, and raising kids, as the saying goes, "is like being pecked to death by a chicken." Thus, the human female is a bit more discriminating when it comes to choosing a partner in the quest for immortality. The male doesn't have that challenge; he can hit and run, which often happens. Our elders have known about the "ways of men" for thousands of years and many rules and rituals have been concocted mainly to keep stress down and, perhaps more importantly for sedentary people, to know who is family, to whom one is related and/or obligated. In the West, marriage ceremonies, mortgages, and car payments act as glue in our culture, in hopes of maintaining the male/female bond, but the glue is "water soluble." I will add that the male/male and the female/female bonds seems to be much more durable.

Some morality is created by culture but there are certain behaviors that must be restricted or the group can't function. Emotional and physical abuse, along with lying, cheating, bearing false witness, stealing, are socially disruptive. In fact, one of the first restrictions regarding sex might have been rape, an act of violence, which could be avoided, in large measure, by restricting interaction between men and women in some manner. Having women's work and men's work would be one way of keeping the sexes apart, enhancing the male/male bond (until recently this was the norm at least in Western culture); the "men's house" might represent another. Specific rituals, however, would serve to bring males and females together.

Third Triad

Rules – There are two general types of rules, explicit and implied. Explicit rules are those we negotiate, or at least our ancestors did, and then passed them down to the next generation. Implied rules are quite different. An implied rule occurs when you do something, it is allowed, and over time it becomes expected. Implied rules help cultures "self-assemble" (see Rush 1996). Implied rules, however, can be destructive because they are difficult to renegotiate. As an example, a gal meets a guy, they have fun. He gets together on Sundays with the boys, drinks beer, and roots for the team. The gal has dinner with her parents every Sunday, without fail, a perfect situation for her. There is no judgment about the guy's "boys' night out," and there is no judgement regarding family ties. Time goes on, marriage is proposed, and the ceremony occurs. Six months into the marriage, the now husband (no longer a boyfriend) is enjoying Sunday with the boys, and the wife spends Sunday dinner at the parents. Of course, the parents wonder about this, not realizing that an implied rule is in play, that is, the husband's need to continue the rules in his former role. He is confronted by the wife, "I want you to spend Sunday afternoon and evenings with the family!" The response by the husband, who didn't get the rules for the husband role, is, "What? This is what I've always done! Ah, the boys were right, you're trying to change me! I'm leaving!" Out the door he goes, back home to Mama. Implied rules can be devastating to a relationship especially when changing roles, as all role sets come with behavior rules and consequences.

Roles – In most human groups, with the exception of industrialized nations with welfare systems, everyone has a job description, based on age (a two-year-old can't do what a 12-year-old can do), or whether male or female (women are better at certain tasks than men and vice versa). What *ascribed* roles do is help maintain order and expectations. Achieved roles, however, are also surrounded with ritual, whether this be a graduation ceremony, obtaining a higher grade in the Freemasons, or becoming a member of the House of

Representatives. Roles can also confer power, the power to make decisions that can affect millions of people.

Anthropologists assume that in earlier, hunter/gathering groups everyone had a job, everyone contributed to the survival of the group. There was also the idea that our ancestors were quite brutal, especially toward outsiders. But, in the 1960s, with all the liberation movements, the old story of the "killer ape" was abandoned for a gentler ape with a great deal of equality between males and females, although this may not be correct either. With primates, especially gorillas and chimps, there are always alpha males, and alphas tend to be bullies. So, inequality between the sexes was probably there from the beginning. In order to change this, you would most likely have to have a language, one that would allow storage of symbols to be transmitted and understood between group members. I think the development of language must have happened prior to leaving Africa. There had to be rules and roles, tradition, if you will, before any sense of survival in foreign lands would be possible and having language would be very important in term of instilling rules *before* there is conflict; just like the cells in your body, thinking ahead has great survival value.

In any case, starting around 50 KYA it seems that human populations increased until around 10,900 BCE when a comet apparently wiped out large groups of people, essentially destroying the developing cultures in different areas of the world, for example Europe and Eurasia. A site called Jerf el-Ahmar, Syria (which is now under water) appears to be a settlement of hunter/gathers possibly supplying labor to the building of Göbekli Tepe, with a beginning building date c. 11,000 BCE. These settlers may have been practicing limited agriculture (perhaps the shaman growing cannabis) along with hunting/gathering. This site supported more than a small group, and there may have been enough calories in the surrounding areas to support several hundred or so people. Agricultural development and animal husbandry in the Middle East didn't happen overnight. It was a gradual process occurring over the course of hundreds of years. The gathering of large numbers of people to help build sites (like Göbekli Tepe) may have been the staring off point for the development of agriculture, rather than agriculture beginning with small groups and then attracting others.

Göbekli Tepe, a site in Turkey dated to between 11,000 BCE to 8000 BCE, is interpreted by archaeologists as some type of ceremonial center and perhaps a cosmic observatory. There are many sites in Turkey that suggest hunter/gathers coming together into large groups. We see this at Çatalhöyük, located a couple of hundred miles west of Göbekli Tepe and dated to c. 7,400 (perhaps older) to 5,700 BCE, and occupied by around *8000* inhabitants (see Biscaglia 2020: 113; also see Sweatman 2019)! This is the beginning of agriculture but this seems like a lot of people for beginning such an adventure. Sedentary living, that is, settlements of hunter/gatherers, not agriculturalists, may extend back before the end of the last ice age (c. 14 KYA). In any case what we see at Göbekli Tepe, the megalithic architecture, the symbols, and so on, likely existed prior to the mini ice age called the Younger Dryas, brought on by comets hitting Earth. The point. With that many people, pulled together into a small area, "equal" won't work. At the very least you need someone to negotiate disputes, for they will surely arise given our small group nature. A prime candidate for this would be an elder or more likely a group of elders, perhaps shamans. In order for such a large system to work you need lots of rules, organization, and *sanctioned power* to uphold rules. There would also be specialists (artists and stone workers, for example), probably assigned some status above that of the average person, and ritual, lots of ritual and mythic ancestors/entities, reference points to bond the members together. We don't know the status of women in such systems, but at Göbekli Tepe, so far, only one image of a female is depicted (there is a great deal more to excavate), probably representing fertility, but lots of male images. This suggests a lower or at least different status for women but we don't know this for sure and we don't know how women were treated.

We definitely see the male energy more prominent (i.e. inequality) when hunter/gatherer groups raided into agricultural communities – male sex bias shows up in the genomic signature (see Reich 2018: 234-235), and it is still with us to this day. Looking at the world politics this inequality is unlikely to go away for many reasons, one of which is the myth of male superiority which likely goes deep into prehistory, perhaps materializing between 50-20 KYA (or even before), and, like the Jim Crow laws in the US, the lingering attitudes are not going away for many generations to come. Remember, the Darwinians believe in the survival of the fittest, and who is more fit, men or women? Darwin claims it is men.

Rejection – Behaviors that jeopardize the group have to be dealt with, and, depending on the issues, these can be quite harsh. Sometimes members would be banished from the group, which, in most cases was a death sentence, to ritual killing in the form of vendettas or the legal system as in some states in the US, Saudi Arabia, China, North Korea, Russia, and so on. What rejection is designed to do is maintain conformity and cooperation and reduce conflict among group members. Using fear tactics and threats, and gossip and rumor, common in the media and political posturing, are common and all are forms of rejection, of being outside the group. For the most part we control with rejection. Over the course of several million years this fear (remember epigenetics?) of being outside the group, a death sentence, is deeply imbedded in our psyche likely as separation anxiety. So, in this sense, rejection equals death. I don't know anyone who likes rejection, perhaps a few masochists.

Small Groups, Culture, and Myth
So, what does this have to do with our small groups, culture, and maintaining the Darwinian myth? Humans are small group animal; we are not a herd animal like deer and sheep. We get together in small groups when making decisions. You might think that, for ex-ample, the House of Representatives makes decisions as a massive

group. That is an illusion. Yes, they may vote *en masse*, but the vote is determined beforehand, in small groups, the members of which make decisions and then sell them to the other small groups through the "pay for play" corruption that is endemic in politics and large systems in general. All large systems become corrupted, at all levels. Why? Our small group nature and our desires, our needs and wants. Established group members protect each other, lie, cheat and steal for each other, especially if members know each other's secrets, which can be used as leverage. Gifts, of one type or another likewise come into play; never accept any gift you can't repay ("Be careful of Greeks bearing gifts!").

This small group decision making is quite evident in Western politics where small groups make decisions that affect millions of people, decisions that are usually for the benefit of those in power, not you or me. Simply put, myths are designed to maintain the status quo, for example, the Myth of the Elite; outsiders are not welcome, Trump found that out.

The small groups that run the Western world have a vested interest in the Myth of Darwin because it eliminates a power above and beyond their own self-interests. Organized religion can unite people and that is a problem; Lenin was well aware of this when he outlawed religion in Russia. Moreover, those in power have to destroy all the symbols connected to opposing systems, these could be monuments, burning down churches, or even special days of observance. The Catholic Church developed an expertise in this arena, killing and smashing, and this was taken on by the Marxists and certainly Hitler. Recall the Taliban blew up the monumental Buddhas in the Bamiyan Valley in March of 2001. They justified this saying they were "offensive," an expression of emotional irresponsibility. This act actually destroyed part of the history in that area. In fact, the Arabs have destroyed much of their pre-Islamic history, for looking back to earlier traditions, the "good old days," was seen as a threat. Keep this in mind the next time a group in this country wants to demolish images or alter days of observance.

The Myth of Darwin hangs on because the story line suites the needs of very powerful, *small groups* of people in political, industrial, and academic settings. By the way, an individual or groups' power can be measured by the ability to help (give money or support) or hurt (destroy individuals or groups socially, financially, and physically). Religion is a powerful tool for bringing people to action, as we can certainly see with Judaism, Christianity, and Islam, and an atheist in power would certainly consider religion, or any belief in a power above and beyond the human animal, a threat.

CHAPTER 9

Conclusion

ONE striking thing about the discussion of evolution in college texts is the insistence on only one interpretation, one model for the origin of species, the Darwinian position. Science is based on doubt. Science is based on theory and the testing of theories. Science is also based on discovery and the necessity of developing new theories, when old theories fail, and then testing to verify or deny. There is a fear here, as I pointed out (Rush 2020), that without Darwin as "truth" we fall back into the dogma of deities and demons. To even open that door a slight crack invites trouble. Darwinian evolution is not science. The concept of random mutations tells us nothing about how random mutations can magically create codes. Amino acids can be assembled in perhaps infinite ways, but they have to be able to perform work – they have to be functional for some purpose, or used in conjunction with other proteins to perform some task. Although there could be several billion possible proteins, researchers estimate there are c. 20,000 that make up the human animal. "Following the hypothesis of 'one gene = one protein,' there should be at least 20,000 non-modified (canonical) human proteins" (Ponomarenko et al. 2016). They point out that one gene, however, can possibly code 100 different proteins. It would take greater than 13.8 billion years to randomly create *just one small functional protein*. What would be the purpose of constructing *one* functional protein in the first place? What would be its purpose, its goal? It wouldn't be able to replicate itself; it needs enzymes and RNA to do that. It can't do anything without support proteins. Proteins are unstable, especially in the presence of heat. Heat denatures the protein (unfolds the protein), like when you cook a steak. So, in the process of constructing this primal protein it would be subjected to many factors that would break it apart; it would be in a continual state of starting over. In a practical sense, the primal, functional protein would have to develop all at once in conjunction with other functional proteins to perform some task. By itself, it has nothing to do. Considering purpose, the Darwinians fear going there, for in their minds purpose smacks of intelligence.

Of course, there are theories about evolutionarily earlier proteins before we have DNA that could possibly replicate, that is RNA and ribozymes, but how did these, if the theories are correct, magically self-assemble? (See McFadden and Al-Khalili 2014: 277-283 for an interesting discussion on these theories.) The major issue is demonstrating, scientifically, how random acts can create codes that can create functional proteins and complex cells without interference from an experimenter.

Random Mutations or Constructed by the Cell

How can we determine scientifically whether alterations of a coding sequence are random or the product of cellular activity? Epigenetic alterations (which may go way beyond DNA and histone alterations) appear in most cases to be cell generated, with many changes occurring shortly after conception and added or subtracted in response to stress and planning for a postpartum environment. Survival is more likely to occur if the cell has an active part in its own change potential. Life has a purpose and that is survival. Random mutations don't come with a purpose, at least according to the Darwinians. Think of it this way: Which scenario holds the stronger possibility of life's survival into the future, a chance flip of the coin, OR planning, altering coding when necessary, and preparing for the future?

Natural Selection or Going in Circles

The concept of natural selection is a circular argument, that is, it is the most fit who survive, thus those who survive are the most fit. I am puzzled as to why the scientific community would allow a circular argument to stand as truth. Moreover, there is no clear definition of what it means to be "fit." Why does the scientific community allow "fit" to stand as some sort of explanation when we don't have a clear definition?

The Darwinian model states that natural selection can *specifically select gene sequences as well as fine-tune systems*, for example, vision or a knee joint, thus creating the most "fit." If this is the case, then natural selection is no longer random and must be directed by some form of energy.

Science and Academia

Science runs on doubt and discovery, using materialistic science (math, physics, and chemistry) to prove or disprove theories. The research found in prestigious journals is then cherry picked by the academic community when writing texts, presenting the information they deem "appropriate" or politically correct for students at all levels of education.

Academia does not always represent the scientific point of view; in the social sciences this is somewhat of a problem as the study of people, and the conclusions drawn, are often questionable because of evaluator/interviewer bias (remember Margaret Mead and, *Coming of Age in Samoa*?). We try to eliminate much of the bias but, because we are dealing with humans and their egos and assumptions, it is unavoidable. Academic departments have protocols in terms of what is taught at each level, and here a great deal of censoring can come into play mainly because of the beliefs and opinions *of those small groups in power*. This does not mean these protocols, or what is taught, represents fact – Darwinian evolution is a case in point. Students should be made aware of this before entering college or university. Don't be fooled, colleges and universities are not necessarily democratically oriented institutions presenting the "truth," with free speech, and this has to do with power and our small group nature. Remember, all large systems become corrupt from the top down in time; this is because of our small group nature, the bonds that are created, and the needs of these small groups. This is actually quite normal, although, if we are looking for equality, and quality information, we can do better. If there are two, three, or more sides to a story, present them all and let the student pick the one most reasonable or scientific. One of the worst things I see in education is a student leaving high school or college/university thinking he or she has learned the "truth." "Truth" tends to change according to the needs of those in power.

Scientists, for the most part, are in search of why and how events occur. On the other side, academics tell stories and they tell many of their stories as truth, without critical thinking, and without also informing, in most cases, that our "truths" are subject to change. I taught anthropology for over 50 years and saw the stories come and go and what we were to believe came from those in some assumed position of authority. In the late 1990s I began telling students to engage critical thinking regarding the stories I was relaying, about genetics, about primate relationships, dating methodology, essentially everything in biological anthropology. A good scientist is always skeptical, like when Svante Pääbo (2014) was skeptical of the results indicating interbreeding with Neanderthals. He had the staff redo all the tests several times before he was satisfied with the results. I'm skeptical of many of theories and evidence presented in biological anthropology, from dating methods, genomic relationships, and who resides at the base of the family tree. My skepticism is well deserved especially when academics outright refuse to consider alternative interpretations or ignore those who do. A case in point involves Madelaine Bohme (2020). She and her group contend that the cradle of humanity may not be Africa and that the older "regional development" hypothesis might apply. Researchers have evidence of stone tools and cut marks on bone found in Masol in the Punjab (Northern India) dating to c. 2.6 MYA and in China c. 2.5 MYA, with the oldest known stone tools found in Kenya, Africa, dating to 3.3 MYA. So, how do we interpret this? Is it all out of Africa? How much back migration occurred due to climate change and the expanding and contracting of the desert that separates Africa from Europe and Asia (Savannahstan)? Are the tools found in these Asian locations independent invention, or was there exchange of information between the Eurasian and African hominins? Where did bipedalism first begin, Africa or Eurasia, or was this an "independent invention" as well? We really don't have answers to these questions because the data supporting one conclusion or another isn't available. The major point is there are two competing stories as to the hominin (biped) origins of our family tree. The standard classroom mantra is Africa (Darwin suggested this), but there is evidence to the contrary from Europe and Asia.

My hope is that some textbook author in anthropology or biology will at least present the new information/research in epigenetics, symbiosis, hybridization, and endocellular selection ("directed mutation") along with the materialistic science that supports these findings. On the other side, present the Darwinian hypothesis, and the materialistic science that supports it. This would be a very short chapter as I cannot find, other than anecdotal "evidence," the science behind Darwinism. On the other hand, there is a great deal of evidence for epigenetics, symbiosis, hybridization, and endocellular selection. Present the stories and the evidence that supports both positions. Let the students decide which position is more reasonable for the origin of species. At the very least, if these authors can't break away from Darwin show students how random mutations can create codes, without researcher interference, and how natural selection can select specific traits and fine-tune them using a precise definition in terms of what it means to be "fit." Anecdotes do not pass as science.

Endocellular Selection – Too Slow for Complex Lifeforms

Once we consider, or rather admit that cell's think, make decisions, and alter their genetic coding accordingly, we can see how, influenced by the *same* stressor (predator, nutritional, cold, heat), group members alter the *same* genetic coding sequences – we see this in the Dutch Hunger studies (Rush 2020: 62-66) and rats (Marchlewicz et al. 2020: 7). The alteration(s), then, that might lead to adaptation in the future is part of the *group* genome, so it doesn't matter who mates with whom, or whether an individual is removed from the "gene pool" prior to procreating – the changes to the coding sequence(s) will go marching on. In this case the external stressors (Nature) select nothing and have little to do with selecting for fitness; stressors only offer possibilities, adversities to which the *cell* adapts.

Endocellular selection and alterations in coding sequences, at least in terms of building a new species, is a relatively slow process. We have a default system composed of bacteria, viruses, and various fungi, and continually starting over, because of catastrophic events as shown in the geological record, is not the best formula for life's continuance. A better scenario is to purposely alter our coding sequences in order to stay ahead of Nature and those inevitable environmental disasters. We "artificially" alter our coding sequences with immunizations; we know that certain foods and pharmaceutical drugs can epigenetically alter sequences. To realistically get off this planet and explore other worlds – if we do not, we will surely die off as a species – we must prepare the body for dealing with UV radiation and cosmic rays (tougher skin, for example). We could use a third or fourth eyelid to likewise protect us from radiation. Our bones need to maintain calcium along with maintenance of muscle strength. We need to be able to store calories without running the risk of diabetes, control stress chemicals, retain moisture without risking constipation, alter nutritional needs, go longer intervals without the need for oxygen, and, obviously, we need more brain power.

We have demonstrated the ability to recreate our *environments* (space ships, space suits, etc.) to protect us from the adversities of outer space, but settling other worlds suggests a world just like ours and this is highly unlikely. If a planet (or moon) can sustain life, the existing lifeforms, the bacteria and viruses, will be foreign to us; this is an enormous problem.

Moreover, humans have trouble getting along with one another on planet Earth, mainly due to our small group nature, genetic pre-dispositions, and egos, and it is unlikely to change when we commit ourselves to living on other worlds. I'm not sure there is a way to fix this without giving up our individuality and creative spirit.

For now, we need to get on with research into life's origins (this requires understanding quantum biology) as well as origins of species, and maintaining the Myth of Darwin does not support science and discovery, only the elite with an agenda. Until the Darwinians prove their case, that random mutations and natural selection are the keys (or keys at all) to the origin of life and species, Darwin's position remains a hypothesis and nothing more. So, as asked earlier, do you want to be a scientist or a politician?

Bibliography

Alvarez-Lario, B. and Macarron-Vicente, J. 2015. "Uric Acid and Evolution." *Rheumatology*, Vol. 49, Issue 11: 2010-2015.

Anderson, D., Hughes, D., and Roth, J. 2011. The Origin of Mutants under Selection: Interactions of Mutation, Growth, and Selection." http://rothlab.ucdavis.edu March.

Aron, J. and Grossman, L. 2013. "mars Trip to Use Astronaut Poo as Radiation Shield." *NewScientist*, March 1.

Biscaglia, C. 2020. *12,794 Yeas Ago: The Visitors of Göbekli Tepe. Las Vegas, NV: Amazon.*

Bohme, M. 2020. *Ancient Bone: Unearthing the Astonishing New Story of How We Became Human*. Berkeley, CA: Greystone Books.

Cairns, J., Overbaugh, J., and Miller, S. 1988. "The Origin of Mutants." *Nature*, Vol. 335, pgs. 142-145.

Campbell, J. 1973. *The Hero with a Thousand faces*. NJ: Princeton University Press.

Carroll, S. 2019. *Something Deeply Hidden: Quantum Worlds and the Emergence of Spacetime*. NY: Random House.

Carter, L., Tamashiro, K., and Pearson, K. 2020. "Maternal Diet and Exercise: Influences on Obesity and Insulin Resistance." In, *Nutrition and Epigenetics*, eds. E. Ho and F. Domann, NY: CRC Press.

Chandar, N. and Viselli, S. 2019. *Cell and Molecular Biology*, 2nd Edition. NY: Wolters Kluwer.

Chen, W., Muftuoglu, M., and Wu, R. 2020. " Selenium and Epigenetic Effects on Histone Marks and DNA Methylation." In, *Nutrition and Epigenetics*, eds. E. Ho and F. Domann. NY: CRC Press.

Cheng, W., Muftuoglu, M., and Wu, R. 2020. "Selenium and Epigenetic Effects on Histone Marks and DNA Methylation." In, *Nutrition and Epigenetics*, eds. E. Ho and F. Domann, NY: CRC Press.

Claycombe, K., Zeng, H., and Combs, G. 2020. "Dietary Effects on Adipocyte Metabolism and Epigenetics." In, *Nutrition and Epigenetics*, eds. E. Ho and F. Domann. NY: CRC Press.

Cole, M. 2020. *Unifying Microbial Mechanisms: Shared Strategies of Pathogenesis*. NY: CRC Press.

Dawkins, R. 2006 (orig. 1976). *The Selfish Gene*. NY: Oxford university Press.

Dawkins, R. and Wong, Y. 2017. *The Ancestor's Tale*. London, UK: Weidenfeld & Nicolson.

Fleming, G. and Scholes, G. 2015. "Quantum Biology: Introduction.", In, *Quantum Effects in Biology*, eds. M. Mahseni, Y. Omar, G. Engel, and M. Plenio. NY: Cambridge University Press.

Freud, S. 1990 (orig. 1913). *Totem and Taboo*. NY: W. W. Norton and Co.

Ho, E. and Domann, F. eds. 2020. *Nutrition and Epigenetics* NY: CRC Press.

Hoffman, D. 2019. *The Case against Reality: Why evolution hid the Truth from Our Eyes*. NY: W. W. Norton & Company.

Johnson, R. and Andrews, P. 2011. "Fructose, uricase, and the Back-to- Africa hypothesis." *Evolutionary Anthropology*, January.

Kaku, M. 2021. *The God Equation: The Quest for a Theory of Everything*. NY: Doubleday.

Kenyon, G. 1986. "Forward." In, C. Thaxton, W. Bradley, and R. Olsen, *The Mystery of Life's Origin: Reassessing Current Theories*. NY: Philosophical Library.

Kenyon, G. and Steinman, G. 1969. *Biochemical Predestination*. NY: McGraw-Hill.

Kim, Y., Bertagna, F., D'Souza, E. et al. "Quantum Biology: An Update and Perspective." *Quantum Reports*, 3(1), 80-126.

Krauss, L. 2013. *A Universe from Nothing: Why There is Something Rather than Nothing*. NY: Simon & Schuster.

Lamarck, J. 1809. Philosophie Zoologique, ou Exposition des considerations relatives a l'histoire naturelle des animaux (Zoological Philosophy: or Exposition with Regard to the Natural History of Animals).

Lanza, R. 2020. *The Grand Biocentric Design: How Life Creates Reality*. Dallas, TX: BenBella Books.

Li, Y. and Zhang, Y. 2014. "DNA Methylation in Mammals." *Cold Spring Harbor Perspective on Biology*, May: 6(5)

Lieff, J. 2020. *The Secret Language of cells: What Biological Conversations Tell Us About the Brain-Body Connection, the Future of Medicine, and Life Itself*. Dallas, TX: BenBella Books.

Malinowski, B. 1927. *Sex and Repression in Savage Society*. London: Routledge & Kegan Paul, Trench, Trubner.

Malinowski, B. 1929. "Kinship." *Encyclopedia Britannica*, 14th edition, Vol. 13: 403-409.

Marchlewicz, E., Anderson, O., and Dolinoy, D. 2020. "Early-Life Exposures and the Epigenome: Interactions between Nutrients and the Environment." In, *Nutrition and Epigenetics*, eds. E. Ho and F. Domann, NY: CRC Press.

Mahseni, M., Omar, Y., Engel, G., and Plenio, M., (eds). 2015. *Quantum Effects in Biology*. NY: Cambridge University Press.

McFadden, J. and Al-Khalili, J. 2014. *Life on the Edge: The Coming of Age of Quantum Biology*. NY: Broadway Books.

Meyer, S. 2021. *Return to the God Hypothesis: Three Scientific Discoveries that Reveal the Mind Behind the Universe*. NY: HarperOne.

Moorhead, P. and Kaplan, M. eds. 1967. *Mathematical Challenges to the Neo-Darwinian Interpretation of Evolution*. Philadelphia: Wister Institute.

Morgan, L. 1877. *Ancient Society*. NY: Henry Holt, and Company.

Noble, D. 2017. "Digital and Analogue Information in organisms." In, *From Matter to Life: Information and Causality*, eds. S. Walker, P. Davies, and G. Ellis, pages 114-129. NY: Cambridge university Press.

Pääbo, S. 2014. *Neanderthal Man: In Search of Lost Genomes*. NY: Basic Books.

Pan, Y., Strakovsky, R., Zhou, D., Wang, H., and Chen, H. 2020. "Maternal Protein and Fat Intake: Epigenetic Consequences of Fetal Development." In, *Nutrition and Epigenetics*, eds. E. Ho and F. Domann, NY: CRC Press.

Pham, T. and Lee, J. 2020. Regulation of Histone Acyltransferases and Deacetylases by Bioactive Food Compounds for the Prevention of Chronic Diseases." In, *Nutrition and Epigenetics*, eds. E. Ho and F. Domann, NY: CRC Press.

Ponomarenko, E., Poverennaya, E., Ligisonis, E. et al. 2016. "The Size of the Human Proteome: The Width and Depth." *International Journal of Analytical Chemistry*, May 19.

Prang, J., Liu, W., Hancock, C., and Harman, M. 2020. Proline: Metabolic Sensing and Parametabolic Regulation." In, *Nutrition and Epigenetics*, eds. E. Ho and F. Domann, NY: CRC Press.

Prigogine, I, Nicolis, G. and Babloyantz. 1972. "Thermodynamics of Evolution." *Physics Today* 25 (11), 23-31.

Redfield, R. 2001. "Do Bacteria have Sex?" *Nature Reviews Genetics* 2, 634-639.

Reich, D. 2018. *Who We Are and How We Got Here: Ancient DNA and the Science of the Human Past*. NY: Pantheon Books.

Rush, J. 2021. *Cat Tales: Origins, Interactions, and Domestication of Felis catus*. Middletown, DE: Amazon.

Rush, J. 2020. *What Darwin and Dawkins Didn't Know: Epigenetics, Symbiosis, Hybridization, Quantum Biology, Topobiology, the Sugar Code, and the Origin of Species*. Monee, IL: Amazon.

Rush, J. ed. 2013. *Entheogens and the Development of Culture*. Berkeley, CA: North Atlantic Books.

Rush, J. 2011. *The Mushroom in Christian Art: The Identity of Jesus in the Development of Christianity*. Berkeley, CA: North Atlantic Books.

Rush, J. 1999. *Stress and Emotional Health: Applications of Clinical Anthropology*. Westport, Conn: Auburn House.

Rush, J. 1996. *Clinical Anthropology: An Application of Anthropological Concepts within Clinical Settings*. Westport, Conn: Praeger Press.

Schindler, T. 2018. "Bacterial Sex: The Promiscuous Process Driving Antibiotic Resistance." *STAT*, Feb. 20.

Schrodinger, E. 1956. *What is Life? With Mind and Matter and Autobiographical Sketches*. NY: Cambridge University Press.

Shabani, A., Mohseni, M., Jang, S., Tshizaki, A., Plenio, M., Rebentrost, P., Aspuru-Guzik, A., Cao, J., Lloyd, S., and Silbey, R. 2105. "Open quantum system approaches to biological systems." In, *Quantum Effects in Biology*, eds. M. Mahseni, Y. Omar, G. Engel, and M. Plenio. NY: Cambridge University Press.

Shubin, N. 2020. *Some Assembly Required: Decoding Four Billion Years of Life, from Ancient Fossils to DNA*. NY: Pantheon Books.

Sitchin, Z. 1995. *The Earth Chronicles*, Vol. 1-9. NY: Avon Harper.

Skinner, M., Gurerrero-Bosagna, C., Haque, M., Nilsson, E., Knop, J., Knutie, S., and Clayton, D. 2014. "Epigenetics and the Evolution of Darwin's Finches." *Genome Biology and Evolution* 6 (8): 1972- 1989.

Spencer, H. 2017 [orig. 1862]. *First Principles of a New System of Philosophy* . CreateSpace Independent Publishing Platform.

Strandwitz, P. 2018. "Neurotransmitter modulation by gut microbiota." *Brain Research,* Vol. 1693, Part B, August 15: 128-133.

Sweatman, M. 2019. *Prehistory Decoded: A Science Odyssey Unifying Astronomy, Geochemistry and Archaeology*. Leicestershire, UK: Matador Books.

Thaxton, C., Bradley, W., Olsen, R., Tour, J., Meyer, S., Wells, J., Gonzalez, G., Miller, B., and Klinghoffer, D. 2020. *Mystery of Life's Origin: The Continuing Controversy*. Seattle, WA: Discovery Institute Press.

Thaxton, R., Bradley, C., and Olsen, W. 1986. *The Mystery of Life's Origin: Reassessing Current Theories*. Philosophical Library.

Van Gilder, T. and Remington, P. 2017. "Medical education needs to take 'an ounce of prevention' seriously." *STAT* (January 19).

Wynn, T. 1989. *The Evolution of Spatial Consciousness*. Urbana, Il.: University of Illinois Press.

Yockey, H. 2005. *Information Theory, Evolution, and the Origins of Life*. NY: Cambridge University Press.

Index

Author Profile

John A. Rush, Ph.D., N.D. is a retired Professor of Anthropology, with specialties in information theory and human information processing, myth/symbolism, and biological anthropology. Dr. Rush is also a retired Naturopathic Doctor, with specialties in nutrition, cellular toxicity, and medical hypnotherapy. Dr. Rush's publications include *Witchcraft and Sorcery: An Anthropological Perspective of the Occult* (1974), *The Way We Communicate* (1976), *Clinical Anthropology: An Application of Anthropological Concepts within Clinical Settings* (1996), *Stress and Emotional Health: Applications of Clinical Anthropology* (1999), *Spiritual Tattoo: A Cultural History of Tattooing, Piercing, Scarification, Branding, and Implants* (2005), *The Twelve Gates: A Spiritual Passage through the Egyptian Book of the Dead* (2007), *Failed God: Fractured Myth in a Fragile World* (2008), *The Mushroom in Christian Art: The Identity of Jesus in the Development of Christianity* (2011), editor of and contributor to, *Entheogens and the Development of culture: The Anthropology and Neurobiology of Ecstatic Experience* (2013), *What Darwin and Dawkins Didn't Know: Epigenetics, Symbiosis, Hybridization, Quantum Biology, Topobiology, the Sugar Code, and the Origin of Species* (2020), and *Cat Tales: Origins, Interactions, and Domestication of* Felis Catus (2021).